MW00681853

Nine Mile Magazine

Vol 6, No. 2
Spring, 2019

NINE MILE MAGAZINE
Vol 6, No. 2 Spring 2019

Publisher: Nine Mile Art Corp.
Editors: Bob Herz, Stephen Kuusisto, Andrea Scarpino
Associate Editors: Cyrus Cassells, Jody Stewart
Art Editor Emeritus: Whitney Daniels
Cover Art: Detail from a 6 x 10 ft canvas oil painting, "YOU ARE
ON," showing performers' view of the audience. The painting was
created in 1983 by Thomasina DeMaio.

The publishers gratefully acknowledge support of the New York
State Council on the Arts with the support of Governor Andrew M.
Cuomo and the New York State Legislature.   We also
acknowledge support of the County of Onondaga and CNY Arts
through the Tier Three Project Support Grant Program.   We have
also received significant support from the Central New York
Community Foundation. This publication would not have been
possible without the generous support of these groups. We are very
grateful to them all.

ISBN-10: 1-7326600-2-6
ISBN-13: 978-1-7326600-2-1

Poetry and artwork copyright of their respective authors and artists.
All rights reserved. No poem or artwork may be reproduced in full
or in part without prior written permission from its owner.

NEW YORK
STATE OF
OPPORTUNITY.

Council on
the Arts

Contents

About Nine Mile Magazine

We publish twice yearly, showcasing the best work we receive from authors whose work, energy, and vision seem to us most deeply entangled with life. We are deeply committed to featuring diverse writers, including writers with mental and physical disabilities, and writers from different races, genders, ages, sexual identities, cultures, and religions.

With this issue we include new associate editors, the well-known poets Cyrus Cassells and Jody Stewart. We welcome them both.

SUBMISSIONS

For consideration in the magazine, submit 4 - 6 poems in Word or text at editor@ninemile.org. You can access a submission form at our website, ninemile.org. Please include:

- your name and contact information (email and home address for sending contributor's copies)
- a paragraph about yourself (background, achievements, etc),
- a statement of your aesthetic intent in the work ,
- a photo of yourself

We respond within 2 weeks. If you do not hear from us, reconnect to make sure we received your submission. Note that we do not accept unsolicited essays, reviews, video / motion based art, or Q&A's.

TALK ABOUT POETRY PODCASTS AND BLOG

At our Talk About Poetry podcast working poets discuss poems that interest, annoy, excite, and engage them. The Talk About Poetry blog provides more opportunities for feedback. The addresses are:

- *Soundcloud*: https://soundcloud.com/bobherz;
- *iTunes*: https://itunes.apple.com/us/podcast/talk-about-poetry/id972411979?mt=2;
- *Talk About Poetry blog*: https://talkaboutpoetry.wordpress.com

NINE MILE BOOKS

Nine Mile Books are available at our website, ninemile.org, or online at Amazon.com and iTunes. Recent books are:

- *A Little Gut Magic*, Matthew Lippman (2018), $16. "Reading Matthew Lippman's poems feels like having a conversation with a hilarious, brutally honest, and brilliant friend."—Jessica Bacal, author of *Mistakes I Made at Work: 25 Influential Women Reflect on What They Got Out of Getting It Wrong.*

- *The Golem Verses*, Diane Wiener (2018), $16, or $9.99 at Kindle and iBooks. Of this book the poet Georgia Popoff has written, "...Diane Wiener unlocks the door to a room of confidences, secrets, passions, and fears. These poems present an interior dialogue in which the Golem is more than symbol or legend but trusted companion and guiding, grounding force. This room is furnished with intellect, wonder, inquiry, discovery, revelation, and release. Curl up in a comfy chair and bear witness to this lyric journey."

- *Perfect Crime*, David Weiss (2017), $16. Of this book the poet says, "The whole of it thinks about the idea of perfect crime metaphysically, in the sense that time, for example, is, itself, a perfect crime. Perfect meaning: effect without cause. A crime or situation or condition that can't be solved."

- *Where I Come From* (2016), Jackie Warren-Moore, $12. Poet, playwright, theatrical director, teacher, and freelance writer, Ms. Warren-Moore's work has been published nationally and internationally. She is a Survivor, of racism, sexism, sexual abuse, and physical abuse, who regards her poetic voice as the roadmap of her survival, a way of healing herself and of speaking to the souls of others.

- *Selected Late Poems of Georg Trakl* (2016), translations by Bob Herz, $7.50 plus mailing, or $7.49 at Kindle and iBooks. This book includes all the poems Trakl wrote in the last two years of his life, from *Sebastian in Dream* and the poems that appeared in *Der Brenner*, plus some poems from other periods showing the development of the poet's art.

- *Letter to Kerouac in Heaven* (2016) by Jack Micheline, $10. One of the original Beats, Michelin's career took him from Greenwich Village to San Francisco, with friends that included almost everyone, from Mailer to Ginsberg to Corso and others. He was a street poet whose first book included an introduction by Jack Kerouac and was reviewed in *Esquire* by Dorothy Parker. This is a replica publication of one of his street books.
- *Bad Angels*, Sam Pereira (2015). $20; or on Kindle and iBooks, $9.99. Of this poet Peter Everwine wrote, "He's an original." Pereira's work has been praised by Norman Dubie, David St. John, and Peter Campion.
- *Some Time in the Winter*, Michael Burkard (2014). $16. A reprint of the famed original 1978 chapbook with an extended essay by Mr. Burkard on the origins of the poem.
- *Poems for Lorca*, Walt Shepperd (2012). $9.95. The poems continue Mr. Shepperd's lifelong effort to truly see and record the life around him. Lorca is his daughter, and the poems constitute an invaluable generational gift from father to daughter, and from friend, colleague, and community member to all of us.

Nine Mile Magazine

Vol 6, No. 2
Spring, 2019

Appreciations & Asides

Miscellaneous notes gathered from here and there on art, literature, and life, from artists and critics we love or statements we find curiously interesting.

■ OUR UNIVERSITIES SHOULD PRODUCE GOOD criticism; they do not—or, at best, they do so only as federal prisons produce counterfeit money: a few hardened prisoners are more or less surreptitiously continuing their real vocations.
—Randall Jarrell, "Contemporary Poetry Criticism," *Kipling, Auden & Co.*, (Farrar, Strauyss, Giroux, 1980)

■ NO MAN IS CAPABLE OF TRANSLATING POETRY, who besides a Genius to that Art, is not a Master both of his Authours Language, and of his own: Nor must we understand the Language only of the Poet, but his particular turn of Thoughts, and of Expression, which are the Characters that distinguish, and as it were individuate him from all other writers... The like Care must be taken of the more outward Ornaments, the Words: when they appear (which is but seldom) litterally graceful, it were an injury to the Authour that they should be chang'd: But since every Language is so full of its own proprieties, that what is Beautiful in one, is often Barbarous, nay sometimes Nonsence in another, it would be unreasonable to limit a Translator to the narrow compass of his Authours words: 'tis enough if he choose out some Expression which does not vitiate the Sense... There is therefore a Liberty to be allow'd for the Expression, neither is it necessary that Wordes and Lines should be confin'd to the measure of their Original. The sence of an Authour, generally speaking, is to be Sacred and inviolable. If the Fancy of Ovid be luxuriant, 'tis his Character to be so, and if I retrench it, he is no longer Ovid.
—John Dryden, *The Preface to Ovid's Epistles* (1680).)

■ WHEN I TALK ABOUT POLITICAL POETRY, I MEAN that work which is attentive to the way an individual sense of identity is shaped by collision with the collective, how one's sense of self is defined through encounter with the social world. Such a

poem doesn't necessarily deal with, say, the crisis in Bosnia or America's brutal mishandling of the AIDS epidemic, though it might be concerned with these things. Though it does do more than occupy the space of the lyric "I"; it is interested, however subtly, in the encounter between self and history.... In this sense, many of the poems I love best are political poems. Bishop's "The Moose", for instance, is a brilliant evocation of an experience in which an outsider, defined by her separation from those perennial family voices droning on in the back of the bus, suddenly has a mysterious experience of connection, of joining a community of inarticulate wonder in the face of otherness. The isolation of the speaker in the proem to "The Bridge" is not just an existential loneliness; he's waiting in the cold "under the shadows of Thy piers" for a reason, which has to do with his position as a sexual other. That the great steel rainbow of the bridge arcs over him... is no accident; his otherness is an essential condition which helps to create the joy he feels in the transcendent promise of the bridge.
—Mark Doty, interview with Mark Wunderlich, *The Cortland Review* (December 1998)

■ AT FIRST CRITICS CLASSIFIED AUTHORS AS Ancients, that is to say, Greek and Latin authors, and Moderns, that is to say, every post-Classical Author. Then they classified them by eras, the Augustans, the Victorians, etc., and now they classify them by decades, the writers of the '30's, '40's, etc. Very soon, it seems, they will be labeling authors, like automobiles, by the year.
—W.H. Auden, "Reading," *The Dyer's Hand, and Other Essays* (Random House, 1962)

■ IN MOMENTS OF CRISIS, WHERE THERE IS GENUINE trauma, as with September 11, but also with the war in Iraq and as in Vietnam, you see an acceleration in the manipulation of the public language by both the state and the mediocracy. At such time one comes face-to-face with how inadequate the language of the mass culture is, the reports and commentary on television and the newspapers. In such time, the necessity for poetry is all the more palpable – to deal with an ever more complex reality and in a more

complex way. Yet the very complexity that prevents poetry from having a mass audience, from being popular, is at the heart of its political value, contradictory as that is to social realism or to populist idealism. Poetry is political to the degree that it refuses the language of Massed Culture and the Official Religions and Corporate State, while at the same time actively engaging political discourses... Poetry is not a form of macro politics, it's not a form of direct political action, poetry doesn't't change governments, poetry doesn't't stop wars. It's a pre-requisite for political thinking but it's not sufficient form of action. Poetry is not the end of politics. It's the beginning of politics.
—Charles Bernstein, Interview with Romina Freschi, Buenos Aires, June 2005, published in *Plebella*, No. 6, December 2005

■ [A]S A POET, I MAY VERY POSSIBLY BE MORE interested in the so-called illogical impingements of the connotations of words on the consciousness (and their combinations and interplay in metaphor on this basis) than I am interested in the preservation of their logically rigid significations at the cost of limiting my subject matter and the perceptions involved in the poem.
—Hart Crane, letter to Harriet Monroe (in *Poetry*, October 1926); from *O My Land, My Friends: The Selected Letters of Hart Crane*, (New York: Four Walls Eight Windows, 1997)

■ ONE OF POETRY'S GREAT EFFECTS, THROUGH its emphasis upon feeling, association, music and image — things we recognize and respond to even before we understand why — is to guide us toward the part of ourselves so deeply buried that it borders upon the collective.
—Tracy K. Smith, "Staying Human: Poetry in the Age of Technology," *The Washington Post*, May, 2018

■ A POEM THAT CALLS US FROM THE OTHER SIDE OF a situation of extremity cannot be judged by simplistic notions of "accuracy" or "truth to life." It will have to be judged, as Ludwig Wittgenstein said of confession, by its consequences, not by our ability to verify its truth. In fact, the poem might be our only evidence that an event has occurred: it exists for us as the sole trace of an occurrence. As such, there is nothing for us to base the poem on, no independent account that will tell us whether or not we can see a given text as being "objectively" true. Poem as trace, poem as evidence.

—Carolyn Forche, Introduction to *Against Forgetting, Twentieth Century Poetry of Witness* (Norton, 1993)

■ EVERYTHING IS COMPARABLE TO EVERYTHING everything finds its echo, its reason, its resemblance, its opposition, its becoming everywhere. And this becoming is infinite.

—Paul Eluard, *Capital of Pain*, tr. Richard Weisman, (Grossman Publishers, 1973)

■ IN THE ANAGOGIC ASPECT OF MEANING, THE radical form of metaphor, "A is B," comes into its own [and] may be hypothetically applied to anything, for there is no metaphor, not even "black is white," which a reader has any right to quarrel with in advance. The literary universe, therefore, is a universe in which everything is potentially identical with everything else.

—Northrop Frye, *Anatomy of Criticism* (Princeton University Press, 1957)

■ YOU WILL NEVER BE ANY GOOD AS A POET, UNLESS you arrange your life and your values in the hope of writing great poems—always knowing (and if you do not know it you are a fool) that you may well have "messed up your life for nothing." And you will probably feel that in pursuing your ambitions you have messed up the lives of others, or that you have encouraged their destruction for the selfish sake of your art.

—Donald Hall, *Remembering Poets* (Harper & Row, 1977)

■ AND THE SPEAKING WILL GET EASIER AND EASIER. And you will find you have fallen in love with your own vision, which you may never have realized you had. And you will lose some friends and lovers, and realize you don't miss them. And new ones will find you and cherish you. And you will still flirt and paint your nails, dress up and party, because, as I think Emma Goldman said,

"If I can't dance, I don't want to be part of your revolution." And at last you'll know with surpassing certainty that only one thing is more frightening than speaking your truth. And that is not speaking."
—Audre Lorde, *The Cancer Journals* (Aunt Lute Books; Special edition (September 1, 2006))

■ GERTRUDE STEIN (NOT ONE OF THE SLOW WITS) said: "Let me recite you what history teaches. History teaches."
—William Gass, *Life Sentences: Literary Judgments and Accounts* (Random House, Inc., 2012))

■THE MOST IMPORTANT ACT OF A POEM IS TO REACH further than the page so that we are aware of another aspect of the art... What we are setting out to do is to delimit the work of art, so that it appears to have no beginning and no end, so that it overruns the boundaries of the poem on the page.
—Barbara Guest, "Wounded Joy," in *Forces of Imagination*, from the introduction to *The Collected Poems of Barbara Guest* (Wesleyan, 2008)

■ I DON'T WRITE OUT OF WHAT I KNOW; I WRITE out of what I wonder. I think most artists create art in order to explore, not to give the answers. Poetry and art are not about answers to me; they are about questions.—Lucille Clifton, "No Ordinary Woman," *Poets & Writers*, April 1999

■ I AM GLAD THAT I PAID SO LITTLE ATTENTION TO good advice; had I abided by it I might have been saved from some of my most valuable mistakes."
—Edna St. Vincent Millay

■ IT IS LONESOME, YES. FOR WE ARE THE LAST OF the loud. / Nevertheless, live. / Conduct your blooming in the noise and whip of the whirlwind.
—Gwendolyn Brooks, "The Second Sermon on the Warpland," *Blacks* (Third World Press (January 1, 1994))

Cyrus Cassells

from MORE THAN WATCHMEN AT DAYBREAK

More than watchmen at daybreak,
My soul is longing for the Lord
—Psalm 130:6

A MONK'S TEXTBOOK OF SHADOWS

Brother, in the roaring silence
That fills your austere cell,

You imagine that you hear
The busybody world's rampant demons;

Well, I've got your demons:
Truth-teller, God-seeker, listen,

You don't have to study
Break-spirit lynching trees

Or the Trail of Tears
(Foot sores and fever blankets,

Swamps and insolvent treaties) to quail
At the long, abominable spell

Of inglorious shadow,
At the brutish deputy in us,

The lack-love warrior who clamors
For the spilled blood of others

And heralds it as newfound wine—

WINTER ABBEY WITH VENUS RISING

Pilgrim, under in-a-rush chevrons
Of restless desert clouds,

At shape-shifting winter's onset,
Picture the Benedictines' elating valley,

Its eminent gusts yielding
A Yuletide jackpot of curt,

Valedictory leaves—whirling, marshaling
In windswept cardinal directions:

Broadcast realm of *glory be*, insurgent
Kingdom of *kyrie eleison*—

Solstice: a slowly ascending,
Bold as a horseman sun

Burnishes each antediluvian cliff,
Each telltale winter crest,

With its equalizing gaze:
A resolute, dispassionate topaz—

Far from the deriding republic,
A mint-new Herod's decrees,

The poignant bronze of reed beds,
The strict rhythm of the liturgical hours,

And later, as irrepressible Venus rises,
Consecrating the far-flung abbey,

And the stalwart compass star appears,
The ink of darkened, sacramental banks

With pallid embroideries of ice,
The blessed Jerusalem of the pewter river—

ACCEPTING THE PEACE OF SAINT FRANCIS
HERMITAGE

Listen, out of love and goodwill,
I was given a hermitage—

From the prior's hand, a choir stall
Of layered terracotta cliffs to contemplate,

To venerate: *Benedictus qui venit*
In nomini Domini,

Benedictus qui venit . . .
A cusp of inchoate vermilion

And liberating blue,
An umber ribbon-length, imagine,

Of rustic, unpaved road,
Ushering my winter-proof boots

Past grazing ruminants and the lissome river's
Glitter and meander—

Dear beneficent prior,
Will I find impartial God

In the timeworn mountains that cradle
Cassiopeia and Cygnus, The Great Swan?

Will I learn to embrace the wind-blessed
Peace and serenity of Saint Francis?

In the breeze-plied December abbey,
Under the Dipper seeker,

Each midnight now I'm seized
By the imperial Milky Way,

The mainstay Seven Sisters,
Ruby-rare ornaments, gleaming in the brisk

Cauldron of the river's buffeted mirror—

MONASTIC SILENCE

Listen to the unstoppable Chama's
Roaring missive,

The arresting hawk's cry,
The clanging bell at starry vigils—

Then sere, demanding
Ghost town in the Wild West silence—

Deep as a dilapidated well,
Door-closing silence—

The vast scapular,
The sable cloak of night—

Clapper-less silence:
Monk's paramour,

Soul's rosary,
Saint's reliable stratagem—

Here comes the rallying cry of the wild,
Spinning weathervane,

The canyon storm's alarum,
Quick, harridan rain claiming

A deep-carved arroyo,
Then sheriff-fierce,

Swift-footed silence,
The see-no-evil,

Hear-no-evil,
Speak-no-evil denouement,

The red desert *deus ex machina*,
The tight-lipped auto-da-fé—

Silence, silence, silence
Passing any human design,

Bellowing silence.

CELESTIAL PRAYERS

As Christ in his desert crucible
Became brother to the limitless, starry sky,

There's never a lucent night
In the outlying hermitage

When I'm not a loyal son
Or a besotted cousin

To all-centering Polaris,
Show-offy Sirius, and The Northern Cross—

Listen, on my tenth birthday, I was taught,
By my meticulous captain father,

The sundial's impetus,
The equator's pivotal role,

And the passkey beauty
Of springtime constellations—

In the cricket-praised valley,
Where witching hour or wolf's hour

Clarity is the reigning king,
Sometimes I dream

Of opening my mendicant mouth
(Delicate as a gilded carp's

Or a leaping dolphin's rictus),
And letting the unfailing night

Feed me its impossible provender
Of planets and prodigal stars,

Or keener, better, richer:
Bless me with celestial prayers.

DIARY OF A PENTECOST SUNDAY

A brazen hummingbird's flurry,
Its side-swiping motor at my breath—

Ready-to-dazzle dragonflies spotted
Near the Saint Augustan of Canterbury hermitage,

And, all at once,
A quicksilver heron skimming

The fleet, mutable river's hem—

*

Comes Pentecost, with its leitmotif of fire
And rushing wind,

Of springtime babel
And cut-to-the heart communion—

Revealing adept Christ's return
To his still-grieving disciples,

All believers, all witnesses
To the brutal cross

And to doleful, prostrate Mary—
Pentecost: a protean heat,

An earnest gust magically toppling
Imposing barriers between

The manifold earth's competing languages—

*

On an almost butter-yellow Pentecost morning,
I wake to four gadabout monastery horses,

Grazing and boldly neighing
Right beneath my bedroom sill;

Here's the mahogany force of Montana,
The most affable roan;

As I leave the Saint Augustan hermitage
And lean over the adobe fence,

He gallantly poses, with his long, pert neck,
As if on command,

And lowers to accept
My May-time plum and Gala apple:

The warmth of my surrendering fingertips,
The fire of my own precipitous giving,

The cooling fruit, believer, unbeliever,
The word of a festive, luminous language—

*

At Pentecost mass, Father Chrysostom cites
Thomas Merton's experience of oneness

In an unremarkable Kentucky mall,
And I recall my own such mystical moments

Occurred in a dusty train station anteroom
And in a bustling burger-and-fries diner,

When the vibrant strings of the logos,
The vast puppet master, began to shine,

And only connection,
Only abiding union was revealed—

Though most Sundays all we have on earth
Is subjectivity: this tensile,

Two-pronged language of duality,
This tattoo of I-and-Thou—

*

The pearl of communion means
For my longtime friend, a poet,

Three oracular horses in an unassuming field:
Fresh vision that ferried him back

To "the cold womb at the heart of nothing."

*

After the intricacies and rigors of mass,
I remembered the surprising tale

Of my former student,
Who polished the word *glossolalia*

And hailed from an ardent
Pentecostal family,

Yet was queer, God of Abraham,
Queer and found it impossible

To ever speak in tongues—

*

Full spring: the once-spare desert valley
Costumed in voluble greens

And showboat yellows—
Now, suddenly, the nave blue,

Eggshell, and fork-silver palette
Of the invigorating sundown sky—

*

Everywhere spring's preponderant
Green flames, and now,

After satisfying Sunday vespers, the soft
"Peace be with you" of the first peony

That the black-robed prior plucks
And brings to me from the cloister garden.

SINERA CEMETERY

I
Down stream-paths coursing
through vine-and-fennel-laden hills,
the parting sun's chariot sweeps—
through hills, so unforgettable.
I'll pass through a hall
of cypresses,
so green, immobile above
the hushed sea.

II
Behold how my small homeland
surrounds Sinera Cemetery.
Pine-and-vineyard-adorned hills,
the sea,
the dust of dried-up streams.
I love nothing, save
a cloud's migrant shadow.
The slow memories of days
lost forever.

III
Bereft of names and symbols,
beside the mourning trees,
beneath a bit of sandy,
rain-stiffened dirt.
Let the wind scatter
ash in boats
and fine-drawn furrows,
marring Sinera's
April clarity,
my homeland's light
perishing with me,

as I ponder the years,
all that's passed:
odyssey to a terminus
of slow twilights.

IV
Already my eyes can do little
save ponder years and suns
gone by. I can still hear
old carriages wheeling
through Sinera's dessicated streams!
From memory
come smells of a sea
watched over by bright summers.
The rose I once picked
still lingers on my fingertips.
And on my lips,
wind, fire, words already
relegated to ash.

V
Mendicant of old memories,
I knock at every door,
as my useless prayer
resounds through Sinera's streets.
No charity can restore
the bread that nourished me,
lost time. In green solitude,
unfailing cypresses wait
to give me alms.

VI
Spiders spin
regal palaces,

rooms that snare
winter's footsteps.
Sinera's boats
no longer set sail,
for the old sea-routes
have vanished.
The sun can't adorn the ice
with festive damasks
for a sightless man's eyes.
Tiny bells no longer
ring from Sinera's streambeds.
Again, I pass between rows
of cypresses.

VII
Tender grapes come,
courtesy of the hand
of a hallowing silver martyr.
Miniature lights
of processional candles tremble
and spur afternoon's
last rites: viaticum
of Sinera's memories;
to muse on them, I climb
to a presiding cypress.
Moonlight kisses
a hierarchy of peaks.

VIII
Surely rain's coming,
for the peak nicknamed
"Grandmother Muntala"
has stashed the sun in her armoire
of gusty weather,
among her lacy

mantilla of clouds, woven
by Sinera's tiny fingers.
Some bird longs to penetrate Muntala's
prison-cage of light. I ponder
serene cypresses in the wide
garden of my silence.
By the everlasting sea's boundaries
dolphins pass.

IX
Fleeting memories of rain
double the dying flowers' torment
in the delicate, drifting harmony
engendered by the downpour
and the afternoon.
How hushed the sea's become!
And high above it,
Sinera's assailed kingdom, snared
in a sharp-pointed siege:
See, cypresses have culled
the sky's bright weeping
in fleeting mirrors.

X
The arranger of rows
of silence and sorrowing trees, I confer
a magic scepter's serene authority
into reliable hands.
Night, wind, hymn,
ancient bronze forged against
the rain's army,
a harsh solitude confronted
time and again.
Shepherding gods nudge clouds
in docile flocks
to the mountains.

XI
The rain dies
and becomes its own mirror.

Flickering lights lure
    sluggish moths.

A nocturnal wind dozes
in the fields, in the cemetery.
When it wakens again,
      it will be a new day.

XII
Boxwood and a chaste-tree
in an ilex's shade.
Each morning
their leaves shiver
as the awakening wind
surges from the fields.

XIII
Lazing clouds leave shadows
on white cemetery walls
immuring the fathomless
silence of mid-day.

XIV
Crystal-pure memory,
the murmur of fountains, of clear,
ebbing voices.
With dreamy, golden pauses,
I pass the long afternoon.

XV
In local salt marshes,
the cold slow sound
of resounding bells.
Mist and crickets lord
all the afternoon paths.

XVI
Docile-eyed guards go by,
obscuring Sinera's memory.
Night's at its peak,
igniting tranquil messages
of flourishing life
beyond the cemetery.

XVII
O black boat
that docked during my night-watch,

black boat sailing through my reverie
of Sinera's sea!

Now a woman's deeply timeless voice
allows me to detect
a hymn of marble.

XVIII
The boat anchors
in Sinera's peace,
where ancient hands rest
        under ancient trees.

A close-at-hand vineyard's fire
signals summer's end,
as in solitude I await
the lost hours.

XIX
The ostiaries
of an ancient cult open
doorways to the dance
of the sinner and the saint,
amid horses appearing from the sea,
reined to chariots
of black weather.

The wind scatters autumn smoke
on rich marble altars,
on gold-thick vineyards,
darkening the face of whoever walks
the cypress path.

XX
Maple and holly,
secret snow,
the bedeviling *tramuntana's*
thin, chilly air.
Sea-winter: a fragile sun above
deserted beaches.

XXI
Wild, dawn-lit horses
upon a deserted beach.
Drums and voices herald
                spring's nativity.

Later, at the shoreline,
new silence:
chained hours kiss
          wet sands.

XXII
On wet sand
I preserve the balance
of an architectural order.

Subtle, deeply devout,
and utterly resigned
to dogma,
I wrestle with
singular thoughts
along cold, rain-washed
metaphysical paths.

My shattered voice becomes
the crystal of my pain—
Sundays and tomorrows
always the same, the same,
as the April light dies,
and I struggle to stop
the vaulted sky from falling.

XXIII
As the April light died,
and the lyrical daughters
were silenced,
in twilight's hush,
I paced the rooms
of my lost house.

XXIV
No immortalized waves
will be carved out of marble,
nor soaring angels' flights
from imagined empires,
for all at once harsh weather

is here. Memory's voices impel me
through Sinera's people-less rooms,
to the dawn's watchman:
a cypress acquainted
with fiery seas and clouds.

XXV
By the sea, I had
a house, my slow dream.
By the sea.

High prow. Along the water's
freest pathways, the fragile
boat I captained.

My eyes relished
all my small land's
calm and composure.

O how I need to tell you
the rain on the windows
ignites my fear!
Now night
engulfs my house.

Black rocks lure me
toward shipwreck.
Prisoner of my own singing,
all my efforts useless,
who can steer me toward dawn?

At the sea's hem, I had
a house, a slow dream.

XXVI

I can't fight anymore.
I leave you this vast
sepulcher that was once
the land of our fathers:
dreams, meanings. I'm dying
because I can no longer ascertain
how to live.

XXVII

Dreams, meanings, vivid
boats in the wind,
liberty, the enduring word I utter
time and again,
between ancient boundaries
of vineyards and the sea.
I don't rally myself
to the task of living,
for I don't know how. White walls
surround me,
the grieving trees'
gracious, towering peace,
beneath dust and shadow.

XXVIII

This peace is my possession,
and God is my beacon.
I say to the root, to the cloud:
"This peace belongs to me."

From my garden I mark
how slowly the hours pass
before my opaque eyes.
And God is my beacon.

XXIX
The footsteps of a friend
who still envisions
a faraway God:
Are you seeking some name
to stop you?

And with this name,
will you learn
the ultimate secret
of all who've come before you?
Such a lonely man.

XXX
When you halt suddenly,
there where my name
haunts you,
wish for me,
so that I might sleep,
dreaming of calm seas
and Sinera's splendor.

B., March 1944 - May 1945

ABOUT CYRUS CASSELLS

Cyrus Cassells' six books are *The Mud Actor, Soul Make a Path through Shouting, Beautiful Signor, More Than Peace and Cypresses, The Crossed-Out Swastika,* and *The Gospel according to Wild Indigo.* His book of Catalan translations, *Still Life with Children: Selected Poems of Francesc Parcerisas,* is due from Stephen F. Austin State University Press in March 2019. He's a recipient of a Lannan Literary Award, a William Carlos Williams Award, and a Lambda Literary Award.

ABOUT THE POEMS

My poetry has continually reflected my diverse travels. My work is mystical, multicultural, and international in spirit; my six published books, *The Mud Actor, Soul Make a Path through Shouting, Beautiful Signor, More than Peace and Cypresses, The Crossed-Out Swastika,* and *The Gospel according to Wild Indigo,* have been very much concerned with issues of justice, war, conscience, the healing of trauma, as well as the restorative power of romantic and erotic love. In addition to my study of French, Hebrew, Italian, Japanese, and Spanish, I have also been drawn, out of a sense of justice, to endangered languages and dialects, such as Gullah (my latest volume, *The Gospel according to Wild Indigo,* is set in Charleston and the Sea Islands), Hawaiian, and Catalan, which was callously banned from public use by Franco at the end of the Spanish Civil War. I strive hard to make the language in my poems precise, musical, and memorable. My friend, the Paris-based American poet, Ellen Hinsey, once said "poetry is an independent ambassador for conscience: it answers to no one, it crosses borders without a passport, and it speaks the truth." With my poetry, I like to think of myself as an artful and intrepid African-American ambassador working freely and fearlessly in the world."

Dylan Krieger

smiling here to erie

too bad there isn't such a thing as
conservation of grief

the chemicals only spread
the ache only keeps opening its hands

take this—until you're ash and then
regenerate tenderness again again

supplies are endless spinal addendums
to what my pestilence once called

church, a chiming arrest of the cardiac
a frank *i see you*   moon to moon

in the howling house the black bears
share with our particular

feral carelessness i met you
on the steps

and don't pretend you don't remember
what happened next

lakeside reactor

for Jason Palmer

this part of the country is an abandoned nursery full of fermenting
    fruit
sentimental in a deathbed sense, the nuclear plant stands at a distance
i wouldn't call "safe," but it's something, while mount baldy, biggest
    dune
of them all, swallows little boys whole—even ghost towns have
    graves
we hang out sprawled along the center of the state highway, each
of our bodies a yellow line signaling different directions—don't cross
unless you're prepared to collide. beachside we climb up the lifeguard
tower and pass cheap beer and swedish fish back and forth like
delinquent kids—an argument could be made people never grow
out of this, just get paid to stay away, say things like, "i would call
in sick, but there's a 50/50 chance of rain." ok, ok. but isn't it comic?
water keeping you from water. and all those eons we craned
sunburnt necks, reckoning that silver silo to be the spot of untold
castings off, cauldron where all the world's clouds first formed from
    the dust

take the book collection, drink the liquor cabinet

my grandmother was an anvil
shag carpet sanctified by ashes
a bowl of cherries in rheumatic hands

thank you for holding
how may i direct your not at all?
nary a salve for what colludes here in the dark:

alzheimer's
a meticulously organized hoarder
heirlooms putting down roots in nursing home desk drawers

when we cleaned out her two-story condo
i bagged all the classic novels
a brave new world of marooned fly lords and mockingbirds

and my sister and i sampled whiskey, gin, kahlua, crème de menthe
i didn't know how a hangover felt
but the next day, i found out

chuck taylors dragging on the cul-de-sac cement
i said i was crying from the headache—true in part, i admit
but what i really meant can only be spoken by poison flowers in the
    amazonian jungle

i'd pressed my flesh against every wood panel
who would remember my personhood across time without them?
seven swallows flying past the u-haul window, that's who

and all those bound and boiling leaves
packed up in boxes in my brain
about to brew

diaphanatic

psychoactive is the only active, she says laughing
yes, perhaps, but. under the lumber, a buzzard
looks bigger than overhead, so close now
to the grounding dance of the dead that, come
to think of it, it had always been circling, obsessed
with the smell of salacious sheep-on-sheep
vampirism—i pad the walls of the room myself
so you can toss me around without consequence
pretend i'm a see-through piece of lace with
meat trim—sometimes i think my body only exists
insofar as it is carved up and possessed
by your belly, intestines a-rattle with jewelry
ceiling dripping gasoline, at least in this asylum
shit still gets conjugal, lingering on certain consonants
that vibrate chipped teeth like electric shock
it's hot how you chain me up facedown in paper gown
before the two-way mirror reacharound goes sour
but remember: there is always a flytrap pasted
to the bottom of the off-brand grand piano
even when you're not looking or the janitor
isn't posted up on the worn spot on the carpet
picking corpses from its poreless surface
as if the ghetto would be better off birdless

ABOUT DYLAN KRIEGER

Dylan Krieger is a $2 bill dipped in honey in south Louisiana. She collects your lips mid-sentence and sews them to all the other lips of the world. She is a graduate of the University of Notre Dame in Indiana, where she was born and raised, and Louisiana State University, where she won the Robert Penn Warren Award in 2015. She is the author of *Giving Godhead* (Delete, 2017), *Dreamland Trash* (Saint Julian, 2018), *No Ledge Left to Love* (Ping Pong, 2018), and *The Mother Wart* (Vegetarian Alcoholic, forthcoming). Find her at dylankrieger.com.

ABOUT THE POEMS

My writing has long betrayed a personal fascination with faith and doubt, not only in relation to religion and mythology, but also —more recently—the unarticulated beliefs and convictions we develop early in life that may or may not find validation in the more widely held worldviews of our cultures.

Particularly in *The Scar Tour*—from which the poems included here are drawn—I wanted to turn away from the hard-nosed skepticism about religion, philosophy, and mythology that peppers my previous projects, and focus instead on those hopeful beliefs formed in childhood one can't help but still feel sentimental about. While "smiling here to erie," for example, tackles the ebb and flow of romantic hope and disappointment, "take the book collection..." recalls the revelation of discovering my grandmother's collection of classic novels amidst her slow descent into Alzheimer's, and "lakeside reactor" plays upon a surreal childhood belief of a dear friend of mine: that the nuclear reactor outside our hometown was the place all clouds were made.

I compiled *The Scar Tour* just this past year (2018), while coming to terms with what ideals, if any, I myself still believe in, what sentiments aren't yet sediment, after taking account of certain scars and their authors, after railing against dogma for as long as no one knows. If it's true (and it is) that I'm hooked on writing about mythologies, *The Scar Tour* is about taking stock of my own. For, whether "true" or not, self-made mythologies, I believe, are worth explicating. Perhaps that's one of the few ideals I have left.

David Lloyd

RECKONING

Dew, wary of the sun.
Carpenter ant, of the woodpecker's tongue.
Wild flower, of any finger and thumb.

Everything knows everything
or dies. In blindness, the bats
assess my height, width, mass,

loping gate across the grass –
filed in the brain's cabinet
as they ravage twilight.

The doe surveys my gaze from the meadow,
ears and tail up, fawns stowed.

The coyote by the creek lifts his nares –
and I'm digested.

The turkey vulture reckons my age and health –
and circles on high, for now.

LITTLE HEART

A fingertip, the heart
of the ruby-throated hummingbird beats
twelve hundred times a minute in flight

and two hundred a minute at rest,
which it rarely is. No wonder
it devotes a lifetime to feeding the ravenous self.

When this creature mates
with a ruby-throated partner –
three seconds on a thin branch,

their hearts thump faster, louder even
than in flight, bursting, almost,
from nearly weightless ribs.

THE UNKNOWN

You see me better with leaves half stripped,
midway between green and nothing.
My seeds know me not.

The creek and meadow – engorged
while my remains barely breathe.
Squirrels don't mind a bare scalp,

as any branch will do. But birds need refuge
for their antic songs. Ruse of invisibility,
when wind bends limbs and leaves move

like thoughts that must be said.
But not for long. I'm feeling stiff
and can't accept this always-present:

each strip of peeled bark, each bole,
private ridge and notch in the sights of the sun.
My edges have waxed and waned,

adenoids and tonsils long since extruded.
So what's next, you ask, so edgy, you
with the eyes. I'll tell you. I'm not ashamed.

I'll push myself down, that's what.
To the roots, to the graspings
you don't recall, swirling tentacles, subterranean

touches, who knew? though you caught rumors,
though you can recite the muted forenames.
The dark, wet, needy, spongy, hungry, thirsty, reaching

ends of me, tips and hairs, thinnest skin, intimate
with each squirming thumb of a thing,
burrowing claw, blind eye, hundred-legged

cousin, ring-wormed uncle, relegated
to always-shadow, the dead and the dying, yes,
the unseen, yes, the unknown.

SOVEREIGN

The house wren is at home
wherever he is
and won't shut up from the peak
of my roof, foremost lectern in the land,

above my home, as I call it
and can prove to you with documents,
though mouse scat on the counter
and a yellow jacket buzzing death throes

on the sill say otherwise.
But this guy, fit as a fist,
is sovereign over the sky, the air,
the song from his throat,

the shingles that slope away
on either side.

ABOUT DAVID LLOYD

David Lloyd directs the Creative Writing Program at Le Moyne College in Syracuse, NY. He is the author of ten books, including three poetry collections: *Warriors* (Salt Publishing, 2012), *The Gospel According to Frank* (New American Press, 2009), and *The Everyday Apocalypse* (Three Conditions Press, 2002). SUNY Press released his new story collection, *The Moving of the Water*, in 2018. In 2000, he received the Poetry Society of America's Robert H.  Winner Memorial Award. His poetry and fiction have appeared in numerous journals, including *Crab Orchard Review*, *Denver Quarterly*, *DoubleTake*, and *Virginia Quarterly Review*.

ABOUT THE POEMS

I'm interested in the boundaries that humans believe separate us from what we consider to be "the Wild" or "Nature." The curving line of a mowed field, the circumference of a forest, fences we erect around yards, walls we construct for homes – these are all boundaries. Even the terms "human" and "nonhuman" establish boundaries with far-reaching implications. Because of this interest, I have populated my recent poems with creatures that are close by but separate: house wren, hummingbird, cows, turkey vultures, the carpenter ant.

Jessica Jacobs

WHEN YOU ASK ME WHY WE TOOK SO LONG

            I could tell you
again how tired I was then, how
disillusioned. The real answer,
though? I have no idea. But I do know
     this:

          Even with evidence
of recent rain, a desert
says only dryness. Its low bushes brittle,
its cracked earth red as rust.

    Yet this hides the land's precocity
for flooding.
         For after weeks, sometimes
months, of empty skies, when
     rain finally arrives,
     it's repelled.

         No matter how thirsty
the ground, after so long
    without water, it has forgotten
      how to drink.

TO A FLORIDA GIRL, SPRING WAS JUST A POETIC CONVENTION

Having known only Florida's poor translation
of seasons—summer/not-summer—
I flunked my first exam

at a northern college, unable to link *primavera*
to its months; I could name all twelve in Spanish
but couldn't answer that question

in English. Then I survived my first winter
and watched the world return
to color. Girls sunbathed on grass

still cornered by snowdrifts. Who cared that goosebumps
made them a quad-full of chickens
plucked for the pot? After a season of overcoats,

they were so much sudden skin. All of it
a lesson, really, in the value of denial, in how
the delay of gratification can make it, later,

all the more gratifying.
                              Like that one
ice-choked morning in March—nearly twenty years

after my first real spring, six years
after first learning your name—we sat together
in a conference hall, amid aisle after aisle

of unturned pages, and began the conversation
that became our marriage. And when I cradled
your jaw in my palm, I had one thought:

So this is how it finally begins. Spring
for the person who never believed in it.

ABOUT JESSICA JACOBS

Jessica Jacobs is the author of *Take Me with You, Wherever You're Going*, published by Four Way Books in March 2019. Her debut collection, *Pelvis with Distance*, a biography-in-poems of Georgia O'Keeffe, was winner of the New Mexico Book Award in Poetry and a finalist for the Lambda Literary Award. Her poetry, essays, and fiction have appeared in publications including *Orion, New England Review, Crazyhorse*, and *The Missouri Review*. An avid long-distance runner, Jessica has worked as a rock climbing instructor, bartender, and professor, and now serves as the Associate Editor of the *Beloit Poetry Journal*. She lives in Asheville, North Carolina, with her wife, the poet Nickole Brown.

ABOUT THE POEMS

After first meeting, falling hard for each other, then promptly breaking each other's hearts, the woman who would one day be my wife and I attempted to be just friends for six years. But when that period of self-selected exile ended—at an AWP Conference, of all places—we married six months later. My second collection, *Take Me With You, Wherever You're Going*, in which these poems are found, charts that excruciatingly slow build-up and then the rush of those first years of early marriage, exploring what it means to share your life with another person—how it challenges you, and how it changes you.

Poetry Journal

DIABELLI

I'm listening to Beethoven's Diabelli Variations on a windy
    November day when the last leaves are falling from the trees.

Did the ghost trains come through already?

All of a sudden he checks himself as if he'd said too much.

I wanted to buy flowers yesterday but didn't.

When sighted people talk about blind certainty I wonder what
    they're talking about.

About my other side, it has a lonesome house.

Everywhere, directions, possibilities, but still rain at the windows.

Where else would I walk?

I don't like your smile sir.

Up river where they eat song birds.

I'll lend my heart to you but only to make you hear.

Autumn, more ancient than my recklessness....

ODE TO MY EARS

Up river and down—life inside my ears
Ghost-boats ferrying horses
Steam engines spit
Leaves at my feet
Listening without a single body

**

Do you still have them?
The faux diamonds you threw at your father?

**

In the morning
What matters
Is having the right feeling
So the clouds will trust you

**

Ears hold the world's depth
Eyes complain about the candy dish

**

I miss Anselm Hollo who gave me a book when I was 20
Poems by Paavo Haavikko

**

Snowing

**

Today I'm like the unborn
Listening and listening

OLD JOKES

1.

Where do they go the old jokes? The Sumerian howler
—"Something which has never occurred since time
immemorial; a young woman did not fart in her husband's lap."
Up the chimney they go.
It's safe to say almost no one laughs at the residue of smoke.

2.

But we do. Farts. Smoke. Bad breath. The old jokes tell us we ought
to weep.
And poor old Freud who had no sense of humor and wrote and
wrote and wrote about the matter.

3.

"You go first" was in fact the first joke.

4.

When a friend was dying I told her I'd just come up with punch
lines, minus the tedium.
"OK," she said. "Show me."
"I'm not that kind of a pig," I said.
Punch lines don't need support.

5.

Sometimes I think dogs invented the first jokes because of their
noses. We can only approximate dog words. All their words are
hyphenated. Grey squirrel standing in gorse. Muskrat nibbling
on chicory.

6.

Don't forget last words. Oops. The finest epitaph.

I RAN STRAIGHT OUT OF MYSELF...

I ran straight out of myself. I'm certain that's what death will be.
I ran straight into myself. Birth. How it was. Once while on acid I
    saw my birth doctor.
He had eyebrows like antennae.

I ran straight around myself. Like blowing leaves all my selves
    whirling around the street lamp of my body.

I ran through myself more than once, often jacked up on alcohol
    and guilt. My clumsy feet broke the delicate toys inside me.

Down the road, down the road, all my friends live down the road.

Ain't got a letter since I don't know when.

Older now I run to catch up with myself. Mind goes very fast these
    days.

In this life inside the falling a long sweet glide.

**

There was a time when every hour was whole.
Part of Beethoven's wisdom is how he incorporated this knowledge
    into his late quartets.

For my part I have a childish psyche with a porous understanding
    of time.

The child inside me is wishful because of a leaking hourglass.

I've lived my life for my twin brother who died at birth.

The doctor had terrifying eyebrows.

**

I wasn't a poet by choice but by the bardo.

I am however a citizen by choice.

Are you disabled? No I'm a citizen.

The smell of smoke from my neighbor's houses....

Stephen Mead

FOREIGN

movies are mainly my own dreams,
all those subtitles to decipher, line
by line, with the other tongues,
the accents, just another background.

Visuals are the essential book
I am learning to interpret, that great
language of murals passing...

Channeling this, I remember
our sweet salad days before the fridge,
on the table, and you making use
of butter, of fudge sauce, my body
an open tablet, some banquet
for your script of that film written
in skin's fluid.

Now I just dream of that
in yellow highlights with no eruptions
to enter the danger zones, the gorges
of the Hitchcockian cliffs.

There, time's speed cavorts,
& I lose track of the plot-line, lose
threads to blurs.

Waking is just as strange.
Waking is the continuance of a Dali set
in desert hieroglyphs the wind riffles,
but I like the motion's story anyway.

I call to you through it
& your mouth moves its sensuous remembrance

as a drive-in screen in September's drizzle,
that closing of the season

held by a long languorous kiss of French.

UNDERSTANDING SYLVIA

Rooted to rage————
At an early age, Death arrives, sucks
up father. Later, as pollen, he returns.

How to explain it, these Daddies that die,
such evil machinery?

Love, a sensitive nature turns to poems
as a defense, shapes expressions as masks.
For a moment, they work.

Bees become sign language, clouds and stars;
Symbolism. The myth is perfected, utilized
heartfelt. She figures as queen, Ariel, Electra.
Confused guilt turns to anger and fury to purity
though it be but a fleeting paper-puppet catharsis.

Meanwhile there are babes to be tended to, bills,
chores, daily grievances, even pleasure:
Walking the waist high wet, kindness is so nice,
a providence flower, ineluctable.

How to shield what
is susceptible in the face of futility————
Explosions she has nothing to do with, being,
amid Nazis, only a Nobody? Such brutal
vicissitudes validate rage, the words urgent flow...

Life strives to survive, brittle and bitter with pain.
Occasionally something of tenderness, of beauty
seeps through:

Black rook in rainy weather, *with luck...trekking*
*stubborn through this season of fatigue...*Oh
Brasilia...the ancient fear...worries, worries...

This troublous wringing...this dark starless
ceiling...and a heart, this holocaust ...
the world kills and eats

ABOUT STEPHEN MEAD

A reclusive resident of NY, Stephen Mead is an Outsider multi-media artist and writer. Since the 1990s he's been grateful to many editors for publishing his work in print zines and eventually online. Various small ground roots coffee houses and gallery spaces mainly in NY and MA have also been a boon. He is also grateful to have managed to keep various day jobs for the Health Insurance.

ABOUT THE POEMS

Although quite dissimilar in theme "Foreign" and "Understanding Sylvia" are, at the heart, leaning instinctively to the evocative and like an impressionistic painting, hope to leave something of emotional integrity in the heart of the reader. The fact that I am mixed media artist in addition to writer influences how and why I write as if by osmosis. Even if words/text chosen are more narrative than abstract, words/phrases gravitate to me to set as colors to set a musical tone. This is not exactly modern in the 21st century vernacular of social media or even in the every-day-sense of trying to have a conversation, a dialogue, by sharing an accessible sort of confession which could be wrapped up in quotes. Even if I am an anachronism, I do hope the content of what I write, however, still manages to speak to the reader like a tuning fork sort of magnet calling pole to pole.

TRANSLATION OF APOLLINAIRE'S "ZONE"

This poem, "Zone," opens Guillaume Apollinaire's 1913 book *Alcools*. It was the last poem he wrote for that book, and in some ways it inaugurated poetry's modern era in the way it used dislocations, collage, lack of punctuation, and fluid identity. It is a great poem of huge gaiety and vitality, but also of a despair about death—"your Zone with its long crazy line of bullshit about death," as Allen Ginsberg had it, in his poem "At Apollinaire's Grave."

The narrative structure of the 155-line poem is a 24-hour walk in Paris lasting from one sunrise to the next. Its subjects are the things seen and thought about in that walk, including automobiles, detective stories, billboards, a church, immigrants, Jesus, faith and loss of faith, travel, love, and many other things. As he said in his great 1917 manifesto "The New Spirit and The Poets," poetry should include the world: "In the realm of inspiration, their [the poets] liberty cannot be less than that of a daily newspaper which on a single sheet treats the most diverse matters and ranges over the most distant countries."

The poem is written in loose couplets, which I and every other translator tend to ignore, the significant exception I've seen being the incredible effort by Samuel Beckett, who uses rhymes and slant-rhymes in parts of his translation to give a sense of Apollinaire's language. It is a beautiful, fascinating, and to my ear, a not quite successful effort. But it stands well with other good translations of the poem, by Roger Shattuck, Ron Padgett, Donald Revell, and more recently, the highly praised piece by the poet David Lehman. All of these are terrific, but in each I found some bit of language or usage that seemed inauthentic or that struck my ear as wrong. Thus, my translation. I'd be surprised if readers do not react the same way to my effort as I have to the efforts of others, finding flaws in the language translation or bad aesthetic choices made in some of the lines. That's okay. I don't claim my translation is better than others, only that it is different, and that it solves some of the problems that I identified in the work of others. In any case,

I encourage every reader to do his or her translation of the poem. It's the best way to see first hand its stunning beauty and inventiveness.

A few words here about Apollinaire's life: He was born in Rome in 1880 to a Polish mother and named Wilhelm Albert Włodzimierz Apolinary Kostrowicki. He never knew his father or his father's name, but throughout his life improvised a series of biographical fathers, making himself variously a bastard of princes, prelates, a pope, and others. He came to adulthood in Paris, where the culture was then in a moil of reinvention, and became a member of an incredibly creative circle of artists and writers that included Picasso, Jarry, Max Jacob, and many others. He saw, perhaps before many of them, the significance of the changes taking place, and invented the names, pedigrees, and principles for the revolutions of Surrealism and Cubism. He opened his own poetry to new techniques of collage, polyphony, the shifting self (reflected in "Zone" in the shifting pronoun changes between "I" and "you"). In 1911 he was falsely arrested and imprisoned for six days for the theft of the Mona Lisa, an experience reflected in a couplet in the poem: "You are in Paris before the judge / Arrested like a common criminal," and also in his poem "In La Sante." The false arrest was an incident in which his life seemed to him to take on improvisational qualities of fantasy and improbability. (The actual thief was Vincenzo Peruggia, an Italian house painter caught two years later when he tried to sell the painting in Florence.) In a later biographical change, in 1916 he joined the French army for World War I, and was wounded in the head while reading a literary magazine in a wartime trench. Discharged, he returned to Paris, and began a round of prolific activity, publishing erotic novels, fiction, and poetry, editing avant-garde literary journals, writing the play The Breasts of Tiresias, delivering the manifesto "The New Spirit and Poets," writing the poetry collection *calligrammes*. In many ways his whirlwind of activity in support of the arts, the invention of new ways of writing poetry, and his constant effort in publicizing the work of his friends is much like that of his contemporary Ezra Pound. By 1918 he had become the foremost critic of his age, reviewing art, literature, theater, and ballet as a contributor to leading journals and newspapers. In May, 1918 he married Jacquline Kolb in a love-match that by all accounts made bride and groom extremely happy. But his health was failing from the war-wound and the subsequent operations. Only a few months later, in November 1918, two days before the Armistice, he died of the Spanish flu. He is reported to have said, on his deathbed, "I want to live! I still have so many things to say!"

"Zone" is considered by many to be his greatest work. I agree, though I would add as among his greatest works "The Pretty Redhead" and "Le Point Mirabeau," the latter also included in *Alcools*. These are wonderful poems, and share the same robust vitality and risk-taking as "Zone."

I mentioned above that my translation differs from others. I should note some of the differences. The biggest one is in the final line, *soleil cou coupé*, which is difficult in any case to translate, with its non-duplicatable French language pun: *cou* ("neck") is an abbreviated form of *coupé* ("cut"), and as at least one translator (Lehman) has pointed out, the relation between the words suggests the beginning of sun rising at dawn when it looks as if beheaded by the horizon. Other translations of this line include"Decapitated sun —" (Meredith), "The sun a severed neck" (Shattuck), "Sun corseless head" (Beckett), "Sunslit throat" (Anne Hyde Greet), "Sun neck cut" (Mandell), "Sun cut throat" (Padgett) and "Let the sun beheaded be" (Lehman). None of these are satisfactory, nor am I entirely content with my own "The sun now only a half-severed neck," which, though it includes the word associations, and perhaps some of the shock of the original , loses its necessary compression.

My other major change in here is in the treatment of the "flaming glory of Christ," which refers to the halo around the Christ. I reversed that line with the one following in order to make all refer to the halo, and in order to smooth out the English. There are other minor changes, but these are more in the form of choices among options for translations. They are easy enough to discern by comparing this to any of the other available versions online or in books. I hope readers find this translation useful and fun, and that it takes them back to the original French of the poem.
—Bob Herz

ZONE

You've had enough of that old world at last

O Eiffel Tower shepherd this morning the bridges are a bleating
    flock

All this Greek and Roman antiquity has exhausted you

Even the automobiles are antiques
Only Religion seems entirely fresh
Simple like airport hangers

O Christianity in all Europe only you are not antiquated
The most modern European is you Pope Pius X
But what about you whom the windows watch
Too ashamed to enter a church and confess
You read handouts catalogues posters all crying out
That here is poetry for this morning here are newspapers for prose
Here are 25-cent detective story thrillers
Portraits of famous men and a thousand other assorted titles

This morning I saw a pretty street whose name I forget
Shining and clean like a sun's clarion melody
Executives and workers and beautiful secretaries
Pass here four times a day from Monday morning to Saturday night
The siren wails three times each morning
An angry bell barks around noon
Lettering on signs walls and billboards
Shrieks like parrots
I love the grace of this industrial street
Located in Paris between Aumont-Thieville street and the avenue
    des Ternes

How young this street is and you only a child
Your mother dresses you in blue and white
You are very pious with your oldest friend René Dalize

You like nothing so much as church ceremonies
It is nine o'clock the gas glows low blue you secretly leave the
    dormitory
You pray all night in the college chapel
Where the flaming glory of Christ's halo turns for ever
Like an amethyst eternal adorable and profound
It is the beautiful lily we all cultivate
It is the red-headed torch the wind cannot extinguish
It is the pale and ruddy son of the sorrowing mother
It is the tree thick with the foliage of prayers
It is the double gallows of honor and of eternity
It is a six-pointed star
It is God who dies on Friday and rises on Sunday
It is the Christ who soars in the sky higher than any aviator
Who breaks the world altitude record

Christ pupil of my eye
Twentieth century pupil he knows how to do it
And this century changes into a bird and rises in the air like Jesus
The devils in the abyss raise their heads to look at it
They say he imitates Simon Magus of Judea
They shout that he knows how to steal so call him thief
Angels hover around him the lovely flyer
Icarus Enoch Elijah Apollonius of Tyana
They float around the first airplane
They let pass those who carry the Holy Eucharist
The priests who rise eternally in raising the host
The airplane lands at last without folding its wings
The sky fills with millions of swallows
Hawks come crows hawks owls
Ibis flamingoes and storks from Africa
The Roc celebrated by story tellers and poets
Holding in its claws Adam's skull the first head
And the eagle from the horizon with a great cry
From America the tiny humming-bird
From China the long supple pihis
Which have only one wing and fly in pairs

The dove immaculate spirit
Escorted by the lyre bird and the ringed peacock
The phoenix re-engendering itself from its flames
Veiling everything for a moment with its fiery ashes
Sirens leaving their perilous straits
Arrive singing beautifully all three of them
And everything including eagle phoenix and Chinese pihis
Making friends with our flying machine

Now you walk through Paris alone in the crowd
Herds of bellowing buses roll by near you
The anguish of love tightens your throat
As if you could never be loved
In the old days you would enter a monastery
You are ashamed when you catch yourself saying a prayer
You mock yourself your laughter bursting out like hell fire
Sparks gilding the bottom depths of your life
It's a picture hung in a dark museum
Sometimes you have to look at it closely

Today as you walk the women of Paris are bloodsoaked
It was and I do not like to remember this it was the decline of
    beauty

Surrounded by fervent flames Notre Dame looked at me in
    Chartres
The blood of your Sacred Heart flooded me in Montmartre
I am sick of hearing the blessed words
The love I suffer is a shameful disease
And my image of you survives in insomnia and anguish
Always near you this image which is passing

Now you are on the shore of the Mediterranean
Under lemon trees that flower all year
You go sailing with your friends
One from Nice one from Menton and two Turbiasques
We watch in fear the octopus from the depths

And the fish swimming in algae are images of our Saviour

You are in the garden of an inn near Prague
You feel very happy a rose is on the table
And instead of writing your story in prose you watch
The bug sleeping in the heart of the rose

Horror to see yourself drawn in the agates of St. Vitus
You were sad enough to die that day
You looked like Lazarus crazed by the sudden light
The hands of the clock go backwards in the Jewish quarter
And you go back slowly in your life
Climbing to Hradchin and listening at night
To Czech songs in taverns

Here you are in Marseilles amid the watermelons

Here you are in Koblenz at the Hotel of the Giant

Here you are in Rome sitting under a Japanese medlar tree

Here you are in Amsterdam with a girl you find beautiful but who is
    ugly
She is to marry a student from Leyden
We rent rooms in Latin Cubicula locanda
I remember I stayed there three days and then as many more in
    Gouda

You are in Paris before the judge
Arrested like a common criminal

You journeyed in sorrow and joy
Before you learned that the world lies and grows old
You suffered from love at twenty and thirty
I lived crazily and wasted my time
You do not dare look at your hands and at every moment I want to
    sob

Over you the one I love for everything that has terrified you

Eyes filled with tears you look at those poor emigrants
They believe in God they pray the women nurse their children
Their smell fills the waiting room of the station Saint-Lazare
They have faith in their star like the Magi
They hope to make money in Argentina
And come back to their countries after making their fortune
One family carries a red comforter as you carry your heart
This quilt and our dreams are both unreal
Some of these emigrants stay here and find lodging
In hovels in the rue des Rosiers or the rue des Ecouffes
I have seen them strolling at night
Like chess pieces rarely moving
They are mostly Jews their wives wear wigs
They remain seated bloodless in their shops

You are standing at the zinc counter of a crappy bar
You drink cheap coffee with the rest of the losers

At night you are in a big restaurant

These women aren't cruel they have problems
Even the ugliest of them has made her lover suffer

She is the daughter of a Jersey City Police Sergeant

Her hands which I have not seen are hard and chapped

I have great pity for the scars on her belly

I humble my mouth offering it to a poor girl who has a horrible
    laugh

You're alone as the morning comes
The milkmen rattle their cans in the street

The night departs like a half-caste beauty
False Ferdine or Leah watching

And you drink this burning liquor like your life
You drink it like brandy

You walk toward Auteuil you want to walk home on foot
To sleep among your fetishes from Oceania and Guinea
That are a Christ of another form and another faith
Inferior Christs of dark hopes

Goodbye goodbye

The sun now only a half-severed neck

Sam Pereira

POLITICAL ANTEBELLUM

I listened and the cowboy band was okay.
At the start of the next war, we knew

A man's incisors, or a woman's, for that matter,
Would be put to the test every day:

A startled child in the street with a dog
That seemed to honestly love her;

A memory of Southeast Asia, where I never served,
But there, nonetheless, all sweaty and

Bothered by the dark rooms where young girls
Had been forced to give in to evil

In its starkest costumes. Now, a president,
Who, by the very nature of his smallness,

Might, in a moment of jocular oblivion,
Decide to bring in the fireworks during an off month,

Like August, when Americans sweat the most.
He'd been a concern for several years now.

When people prayed, which they never admitted,
They prayed for their old God to take pity,

And cast this impostor, loafer, son of a bitch
Into a fire of some metaphorical significance.

A really horrific blaze, where his eyes explode,
Leaving vapors only the deceptive rich can fathom.

Good-bye, we might say in unison, tanks rolling
Over the streets, their huge metal dicks on display.

Here's the thing: We will never be victims of these
Brutal shenanigans again. Antebellum,

Southern, or otherwise, has been put to rest,
Along with all the other finite disgraces,

In a tower, now nameless forever. It has been
Decided just in this lifetime to be the new law.

The cowboy band just walked back on stage,
Regaling us with horses and gals and petticoats

From the town's general store. The world
Has dodged a bullet; the arts are back in the Times.

Lennon once belted that the war was over. He'd be
Sipping tea, save for a mad cartridge that night.

THE FREEDOM THAT WAS FRESNO

I began to fall asleep
At the oddest times, always
During mid-mornings,
And generally with coffee
Having settled in my gullet.
Thoughts of disease crept in.
Was I, the darkest
Of the then dark school,
Leaving town soon? Were
Ash trees brushing against my hair,
While I took my morning sojourn
Down the walkway to the park
On Echo Lane, trying to soothe
My witless, half-baked dream
Of one day resting again
With Bingo, my first dog,
Who tried and failed more
Than I could ever claim?
Had they been trying to allow
That heaven, if it existed at all,
Be a roadhouse just outside
Of then and always holy Fresno,
Where angels, such as they are,
Rely on souvenir packs of Camels
Beneath their elegant wings,
To hold them up, backbones
Of tobacco, as they spouted
That Lucifer, that beast,
Controlled the only Zippo
For light years. Bingo knew
There was no heaven,
As did my old friend, David,
Who wrote a book proclaiming it
All those years ago.
You die. You go away.

You mention it to the driver
Now driving you both
Off to some ancient eternity,
And none of this, nothing,
Will ever be mentioned again.

A LITTLE STATEMENT ABOUT GUITARS

I remember being the first
In a long line of people
Who would eventually buy
"Blood on the Tracks" that year,
And I remember that it made me
Kind of a pioneer, discovering

The breathtaking beauty
Of what can happen
When genius explodes.
Blood, yes, but the kind
A man might live on for days,
If the moment called for it.

I wrote a letter to the local paper,
Which, in this case,
Was a large university's voice.
I questioned the critic
Who found it banal, who stated
There on page D3, that Dylan

Was again dicking with his public.
What is a public, if not for dicking with,
I typed back, and besides,
The idiot wind was apparently
Not alone in its foolishness.
The critic left me to my music,

There on the bottom floor
Of a sectioned off old house
In the garden district, as yet another
Writer of tunes too clever
To be believed had recently sung
About Louisiana. I finished

My two years of consuming spirits
From morning to night, as some of us do
In the Midwest, while boarding up our homes
For the storm. Shelter. There it was
Again. The Dylan mystique. I drank
To that for 21 more years, before

Lou Reed and I became friends,
While buying guitars one rainy Saturday
In New York. We slept in the doorway
Of a synagogue, while shooting our souls
With despair. This is how you write a song,
Lou says. Critics sample your wares, Lou says.

You put on your makeup and drop by the inn.
No one is ever ready for what's
About to happen. You order the eggs
And toast. You wait. There isn't a jukebox
Alive that's ever going to play "Desolation Row"
When you need it. Not one. Not one.

DOTAGE

for Norman Dubie

Last Thursday My friend
You mentioned in a note
The word dotage which remains
A word that carries on the wind
That whiff of weakened
Formaldehyde coupled with Bardot's
Eau de toilette Two scents
Mingling in the Timothy outside
A darkened mortuary one last time

Dotage I said and then
I repeated the word again
Lifting a lemon water in salute to brothers
It's about stamina after all
Remember Berryman dove into
What he swore to be the sea that day
The snow fell like knives onto his dark coat
And spelled out something to tickle
The ignorance of endings

Clearly in its dotage the snow got it right

ABOUT SAM PEREIRA

Sam Pereira's most recent books include *Dusting on Sunday* (Tebot Bach, 2012), *The Marriage of the Portuguese—Expanded Edition* (Tagus Press, University of Massachusetts, Dartmouth, 2012), and *Bad Angels* (Nine Mile Press, 2015).  He has a been bucker of feed and seed bags, a farm supply store manager, and—for the past 20 years —a middle school English teacher in a small town in the middle of the San Joaquin Valley of California. He is married to the only woman who has ever really given him a reason to fight on. They both believe in the magic of dogs and the brevity of life.

ABOUT THE POEMS

I cannot claim some plotted out journey for these poems, or for most of the work I have done over the past few decades. Mostly, I'm along for the ride, a passenger calling "shotgun" over this bounding glory. So, briefly, here's how I see what finds its way onto the page here: Four poems, some more direct than others, but all trying to cope with certain aspects of existence. Go figure. It's what we do.

In "Political Antebellum," there is no avoiding the potential of Armageddon. It's imperative, however, to wrap a certain dignified grace around the scenes depicted, lest my head explode before saving the documents.

"The Freedom That Was Fresno" allows for a return to earlier times, simpler times, but times where the brew of life was beginning to boil and become non-returnable. There are references made to certain 20th Century literature in the poem, a literature that has saved my life on more than one occasion over the years.

My generation, yes, the one associated with Woodstock, has never been able to tie its shoes without somehow connecting the action at hand to a well-known song or songs. In "A Little

Statement about Guitars," I dive back into an actual moment while a student at Iowa. Dylan's *Blood on the Tracks* had just been released and the music critic for the *Daily Iowan* had written a not so favorable review of it. I remember writing a letter to the editor at the time, trying in my own polished graduate student vernacular to tell him what a flaming failure he had shown himself to be as a critic. Suffice to say, neither of us convinced the other, but my God what a work of art that album was, and is. The poem is certainly less so, but it's important for me to have documented the moment in some way, nonetheless.

Finally, "Dotage." Norman Dubie, a friend for nearly 50 years now, is fond of words like that. He actually used it in a note to me a couple of years ago, and this poem is a response to his note. 'Nuff said.

Michael Northen

DAN SIMPSON, READING

Water laps at the edge of Cooper River,
sun just warm enough to compromise
the breeze coming off the water.
Rain-blanched leaves, broken bits of glass,
twigs stripped of bark, splayed feathers -
winter's final graffiti - rim the banks,
notes-in-a-bottle assuring us
that warmth is not far off.

Dan stands behind the podium
fingers skimming Braille letters
as though to unlock the poetry held there
or perhaps it's an organ from which
his own song rises transformed into words.
At the first clap of hands he cautions:
No applause until the end.
He is taking us down a different river
through bends and cadences he knows well,
our noise like gunfire on the bank
jolts us from the journey.
His voice flowing, honest
opens into expanses of coneflower and larkspur,
not our homeland, but familiar.
It's where we've all collaged our memories from
a childhood prank, a father's words,
a glimpse of heaven.
Dan retrieves the bottle bobbing beside us,
deciphering its hexagrams.
His forecast reads:
The yellow sun shines lemonade
which means the sky must be blue.

ABOUT MICHAEL NORTHERN

Michael Northen was the facilitator of the Inglis House Poetry Workshop in Philadelphia for writers with disabilities for thirteen years. He is editor of *Wordgathering, A Journal of Disability Poetry and Literature.*  An educator for more than 40 years, in addition to adults with physical disabilities he has taught women on public assistance, prisoners, and rural and inner city children. With Sheila Black and Jennifer Bartlett he edited the anthology *Beauty is a Verb:The New Poetry of Disability* (Cinco Puntos, 2011) and with Black edit an anthology of short disability fiction, *The Right Way to Be Crippled and Naked.* His doctoral dissertation, *Disability Literature: Its Origin, Current State and Potential Application to School Curriculum* focused on original research in the new genre.

ABOUT THE POEM

Much like riding on a river, when I began the poem I was not sure where I would end up or what I would see along the way, but there were two aspects of Dan's reading that I wanted to communicate: its physicality and its optimism. Watching Dan read, one experiences the degree to which the body participates in the creation of poetry. In addition, he is one of the few poets I know whose work is not inherently cynical but conveys a hopefulness about human beings. Moreover, Dan's poems are always democratic in that they are accessible and invite you to participate as opposed to so much work that seems about displaying poetic virtuosity or showing club membership. He lets you on the boat with him.

Kenneth J. Pruitt

PARTS OF SPEECH

You tell me that I am your favorite noun
I ask if you mean proper or otherwise
Common you say and I can't believe

that you prefer me over other nouns
like *chocolate   hopefulness   rhododendron*
But what are these nouns but gates

guarding softer things such as safety
the soft safety of a lover's inner elbow
What is your elbow to me if not a noun: *safety*

Plural modified noun: *exhaled breaths*
my own condensation on your skin
skin standing in for shell   *shell* for the sound

of an ocean   When I call your name   a proper noun
into that void   that foreverness

it feels   on my tongue   *floral*
an adjective   It is a preposition
your name   which is *on about around like*

the scientific name of flora which always
startle   and yet feel just right
You a noun   a *tree*   a *center*

Verbs *cloud dance hint* never quite
point to   *add* up to   the language you speak
as the only native speaker of your body
I want to be bilingual

HOW TO FIND YOURSELF

Wide current flows west
beneath the rest flows east
unseen but not unknown

At some wet point they slow
cease resistance and succumb
fold back into the march

in the expected direction
like a sidewalk funeral
where death shines like brass

All this water is a line
to the east   tall postures
to the west   low eyes

All this water is a circle
to the north   trademarked corn
to the south   hungry dust

To heaven we find no beginning
To earth no end in the ground

If spheres are the sums of circles
then rain is a thousand answers
falling in lines onto these planes

UPDATE FOR OLD FRIENDS

I.
Pain but painted with a brighter bluer stroke
Grief but by fingers of thieves I invited
Shot but sharper than bourbon's burn alone
There are lands I have crossed without you

Nations I built ransacked and burned
before the wind gave me a door for my breath
that rattled like machines laboring for war
There are battles I have fought without you

stories I released to the cold blue of January
as your tongue rounded corners with stories of your own
Mine tastes of ash and the fire blames no one
There are flames that have burned me without you.

II.
Watching me fall
across the sky my
plane on fire
like all the rest
like yours Do you
care that I might not
crash somewhere interesting
or might it become
that way because
I crash there

What is the name
of that field
in Pennsylvania

Flames eating upwards
as I drop

burning me upwards
through the cockpit

across the sky that
keeps its blue
clouds that keep
their cotton trees
that keep their green
watch over my street
take the oxygen
mask for myself
hides my face
with children in sight
watching me fall
across the sky
my plane on fire
like all the
rest I once
helped you burn.

III.
In this house all the animals have names
but few speak the same languages

Over time we will learn to share symbols
(for hunger)(for her) made with mouths

We make our fingers into millions of stars
so our eyes will turn them into words

we fill with varying shades accordingly
We determine the color of hope each morning

On the evening our boy feels clear that it is red
he will dream his mind to the brim

with strawberries and amaryllis
In the morning we'll determine it is yellow

and the summer sun will ring his skin
like a pocket hemmed with lemons

Noonday we'll call hope green and he will say
"deep green" He will say "the color my room

becomes when the light soaks the curtains
and drips onto the dim brown floor"

He will say "I have always called that color 'yes'""
I will say "The green of the trees on the city

side of the sidewalk is not quite the color
of envy but it's close"

We'll be done making symbols with our mouths
We will walk into the wash of the sun

done spilling down our side of the horizon
He will say with the shapes of his eyes

that hope at dusk is amber the color
of strong ale wrapping its malts around our mouths

his mouth an open well both a vessel and a starter
made for burning through fires without me.

ELEGY WITH MAGIC
for Alix

your body is a sort of exit
a slowed permutation
grapes disappearing into wine

each beast wild and audible
speaks in their own voice
fires we hear burning

we imagine your mouth open
making lullabies now such hush
like lightning bugs on Georgia nights

green flashbulbs for photos
to catch fairies mid-blessing
like young fruit proud on the vine

ABOUT KENNETH J. PRUITT

Kenneth J. Pruitt is a teacher at heart and a diversity and inclusion professional for a living. Recent publications can be found in *Cagibi*, *Rain Taxi*, and *The Ghazal Page*. He also writes on his blog, Mots Justes, and on Twitter at @kennethjpruitt. He lives in South St. Louis City with his wife and son. He loves what you've done with your hair.

ABOUT THE POEMS

In the span of a few weeks in the spring of 2018, my wife and I had a baby (a first for both of us), and a colleague at the tiny nonprofit where I work died by suicide. All of a sudden, I was reckoning with birth and death in extremely personal ways, even as that reckoning intersected with my own midlife crisis. Often, I feel like my poetics were shaped early in my adult writing life both explicitly and implicitly by older Gen X poets and teachers who feared sentimentality like the plague. I had a lot of emotion I wanted to explore in my poetry and no tools to help with that exploration. Most of the poems printed here reflect that maplessness as their genesis.

My approach to writing at this point in my life is informed by concerns of economy and experimentation. By economy, I mean simply: How can I fit in time to finish this drafted poem and still be a present father and husband today? I heard once, probably in a Poetry Foundation podcast somewhere, that Lucille Clifton claimed to have written such short poems because they reflected the amount of work she could sneak in while her child took a nap. I really get that now. By experimentation, I mean that I'm always trying on new styles as an artist. On the page, my poems do appear very traditional. However, the scattered spacing in "Parts of Speech" or the varied line lengths and stanza structures in "Update for Old Friends" were stretches for me.

As a poet whose writing is not supported by academia in any way, it can sometimes feel like an insurmountable task to gain any momentum or attention for one's poems. We just don't have as much social currency in the bank as others might. We're just working people with families who would find life unlivable if we didn't make art. But thank God for that salvation.

Matthew Lippman

A HUMMINGBIRD OF YELLOW SEX

My wife sends me links to family photographers and musicians.
She sends me blogs of elephant caregivers and painters who believe
    in metal.
There are 400 texts about the color red
and a sizable file on the way Israelis chop garlic and Palestinians
    peel potatoes.
The last voicemail I received from her was 15 minutes long.
She started telling me what a dipshit I was,
and then she started telling me that Donald Trump's facial hair
smells like overcooked eggs,
and then she told me we need a new fax machine
just in case the internet burns down.

Right now I look out the window and there are 2 cop cars cleaning
    up a car crash.
The trees have no leaves on them,
and I can see a banana floating between one building and the next.
It just hovers there.
It's a banana hummingbird,
but there are no flowers for it to suck,
no nectar to devour.
It is what sex looks like.
I stare at it.
I stare at sex,
at the banana that is sex that looks like a penis
and then opens up and looks like a vagina.
It's right there between the buildings,
a hummingbird of yellow sex.
I want to throw away the phone, burn it down,
all the texts and the voice messages, burn them
down.
I want to go home to my wife
and start a fire.

WATERGATE

It's 11:02.
I was supposed to take the kids outside at 10:13.
My underwear is over my head.
I'm trying to sniff out the boy I once was,
my private parts tiny and nutmeg.
I didn't give a shit about Superman.
I was in love with Watergate.
Watergate was my super hero.
All that corruption. That darkness.
Those men in black suits, greasy hair, on television,
who lied and lied and lied.
I'm trying to sniff back into my best form—
the 8-year-old who loved the end of Nixon
instead of taking the kids to
ride bikes that they don't want to ride,
eat melon off the rind like spider monkeys in heat.
I inhale, exhale,
and it's there, that sweet smell of *young boy*,
of Downy, of New York City 1973.
All that dirt and sweat.
It's there. I can smell it.
I take lion breaths. I take hippo breaths.
When I was 8, no one took me outside.
I tossed a rope from the 3rd floor window,
repelled down in my Nixon mask,
met the boys at the corner and blew up Manhattan
with wheelbarrows of Spanish, English, and Chinese firecrackers.
Eric had the Haldeman mask; Karl, Agnew's grill,
and the best one of them all, the John Dean visage—
that mixture of mayhem and music,
of innocence and regret. I inhale. I exhale.
I can't get my kids out of the house.
Get out of the house, I scream at them, my purple boxers draped over
    my face.
Find some trouble at the corner store then get out of it.

Make some mischief then be contrite.
Get lost on the bus and find your way home.
You can do it. I promise, I say,
without anyone getting hurt,
without anyone's feelings getting hurt. It's 11:18.
I was supposed to get the kids outside. But I'm breathing.
I'm sitting here in the kitchen with my drawers draped over my face,
and I'm still breathing.

THE LIFE OF THE MIND KICKED OUT

The mind walks into a bar, sits down, orders a scotch,
a single malt,
pretends it wants to be sophisticated,
looking for something outside
that used to make the inside
feel smart.
But there is no more scotch.
There is no more single malt.
The mind looks around for someone to talk with.
Everyone is either too drunk or too drunk.
The mind is not sure what has these people drunk.
The mind wants to talk Rilke.
Wants to talk Lester Bangs on *Astral Weeks*,
then spend an hour listening to The Lion's Share show in August of
    71,
how it was playful in an e minor chord harmonic groove
that was both an angioplasty hubbub that tried, ever so sweetly,
to quell the domestic turbulence that was outside,
raging on the streets,
between the cops, the politicians,
and those radicalized hippies who, years later,
made fortunes off their facelifts.
For the mind, it's all gone.
The life of the mind kicked out of the brain
into a swellstorm of nonsense,
a shitstorm of howdy doodie dum-dums
pulling levers on Pennsylvania Avenue
that open trap doors.
There go the poor people.
There go the blacks and Jews.
The Mexicans and fags.
The gays and queers,
the transgenders and the transmissions of tenderness
that used to move the mind into bedrooms before sex.
The mind sits down at the bar and orders a street choir

or a bandstand
only to be met with a drum machine and an auto-tune tambourine.
Remember when we sat up till midnight talking bicycles and Beethoven,
how the roving madness of Foucault caught our eye before we knew what to see
and the lilacs made us swoon?
And when they made us swoon, it was then, and only then,
that you took off your clothes and I took off mine.
The mind is talking to itself again
and the bartender offers a Labatt's.
It's all that's left.
Cheap beer and no one to lend an ear,
engage in an ensemble of back and forth.
The mind has had enough and does all that it can to get drunk
then gets drunk,
passes out with its mindfulness on the bar until closing
and then it's closed,
the bar, the barstool, the bartender.
In the morning, curled up against the curb, it thinks:
We used to talk before we made love.
We used to talk for hours
and then we made love
for hours
and then we slept.
It was a good sleep,
a restful slumber,
you and me and the whole country
like anything was possible,
like possibility was your mind and my mind
that made a whole new mind between us
which was a body
that we could reach out, and, if lucky enough,
we could touch.

A UNITED STATES OF AMERICA POEM

The United States is still here.
That's why you have to go kiss your kids before they head out to
    the school bus.
That is why you have to go out to the dead tree,
cut it down,
rip up the stump,
plant a new tree,
maybe a Japanese Maple
because the Japanese Maple is red
and America is still here.
It's in the bedroom, under the bed,
next to the plastic bin with all the summer tee shirts,
the blue one with ponies on it,
the same ponies that run and up down hills in West Virginia and
    Cold Spring, NY,
the ones you rode as a kid
when the air smelled of sweet lilac and burgundy autumn.
You fell off of one once,
landed on America, and America picked you up
like a grandfather who still had his strength,
put you on his knee,
and rubbed your cheeks to make you feel new again.
That America.
It's still here in the ignition of the car,
you've just got to go find the keys and fire her up,
4 cylinders or 6, it does not matter.
It doesn't matter that the mudslide in Big Sur
which crushed Highway One
crushed Highway One,
you can still get America going again,
drive over the stones and smashed trees to the other side
where the ocean goes on forever,
where America says hello in waves and sea glass
and hints at revolution.
You know that revolution,

the one that means well for the guy at the farm-stand
and the gal in the office with the big windows,
the revolution of a man with no home
and the woman with no food
that still believes in the belly of the day,
that there is a word called yes that will lead her to a door
and that she can,
with her last ounce of strength,
turn the knob and walk through.
It's that America that is still here and it lives in your heart.
The one that beats so strong you have to kiss your kids
before they head out for school with the lunchboxes and lunch
        money
and provided lunch service—the apples, the apple juice,
the turkey sandwiches on wheat bread
with the crust cut off.
It's an America for today, the most necessary today,
where Georgia and New York, Vermont and California and Idaho
        and Paris, Texas
have all gotten together like old friends reunited,
sitting at the river on cotton blankets
not talking.
Not even listening.
Just being united states under one sky.
It's blue. It's not red or white.
It's a blue sky
and it's here where it has always been.
You have to believe this.
You have to go outside right now and find it.
It's easy.
Just look up.

THE LIGHT

I spend all day getting ready for night—
the open window darkness that gives me falling leaves, broken
    bottles,
a trip down some potholed street
with no dead end sign though there should be many.

***

All day I rustle the edges of my shirts.
I pack screwdrivers into pouches.
I wind up trumpets.
The voices of the dead have begun to speak to me
with greater precision.
It's not that I listen better.
It's that there are more of them that walk the earth.

I spend all day getting ready for them
and they will never be me.
When I am one of them
I will be a flute from the 6th grade.
I played it terribly
as terrible was all I knew.
Not that I was a bad flutist.
I was not.
But when onstage with the members of the band
I faked the whole thing.
I faked Mozart and Bach.
I faked Jethro Tull.
My death will be a lie as my flute was a lie.

***

I should have been a drunk. A cab driver.

***

Today in my readiness for night
I took the car to the bank at dusk.
I could not find a song on the radio that moved me.
I did not know what I was looking for.
Something sad.
Sad cannot be found.
It has to creep onto your shoulders
and rest its head inside your head.
It has to blow you apart when your eyes are on the road.
I wanted my head to blow up in sadness
but there was only traffic.
In the congestion of rush hour
one must swallow all the exhaust.
One must undo the engine to stay in motion.

***

I am alone tonight.
There is a skylight in the house next door
that emits an orange hue.
It's the loneliest light I have known
and that house is not my house.
It is a field in winter
I stood before when I was a boy
which rose up red and white in the moon
and destroyed the world so completely
there were only the peripheral hills
in silhouette.
They rose into the sky and when I looked back at the house—
my parents inside, my sister, family friends,
bathed in yellow light—
they were farther away
than anything could be
from anything else.
How do I return? I asked myself.
I did not want to return.

I wanted to say *fuck you I love you*
and disappear with that field inside of me,
into that field,
into the life and death of a field
bathed in moonlight before the dawn.

***

All day long I spend my time getting ready for night.
For this moment.
The sky light emitting an orange light that is the moon of that
    house
buried inside an imagined shaggy rug
which smells of marijuana and burnt toast.
The dead don't live there and I don't give a shit.
I live there, in there, in here,
and I am a field.
I am flute and a drunk cabbie driving straight ahead.

***

In night there is a day,
a daylight, a light,
that you can always find
which will be a born thing,
something come out of something else—
a paper clip, a cup of tea,
a box of bottles with the labels rubbed down to glass.
You have to prepare for this light in the light
so when the darkness comes
your solitude is a beacon for others,
for someone's wayward ship on the highway
that has lost its steering, its rudder in flames
that even the concrete can't extinguish.

You have to spend your day so completely upright and on your
    knees

that when night comes
you are there to receive its darkness
as not something broken or dead but, rather,
something that has an opening for you and you go to it
and you enter.

A LITTLE GUT MAGIC

All my old friends are 53.
We all look 25.
I'm serious.
None of us have wrinkles the size of tomahawks.
There are no stretch marks like whales circling the waist.
There might be a little gut magic
but that's due to a donut or two,
some water weight.
I went to the reunion in my mind last night
and all of us glowed like sunlight off of autumn leaves in June.
We were the mash up of seasons.
I sat on a bench with Deborah,
she's the youngest of the lot, and said,
Remember the time when we were old
and forgot how to call ourselves
old.
She said,
We let that go years ago.
Then we held hands and did not mention a thing
except that we were thirsty for coffee and got up to get a pot.
The whole thing got me thinking:
How does the body transpose itself into youthfulness as time
        marches on?
We all have one thing in common.
When we were kids
we ran around naked for hours.
We skinny dipped.
We played badminton in the nude
and sang folk songs till our lips were blue
in the middle of The Pine Woods
but didn't care
and let our voices plaster the sky with tonal deficiencies
but it did not matter,
we were naked and sang like
our songs were the only things that mattered,

like our lives depended on our voices
as they came together
and breathed gold.
It prepared us for tender faces in our Fifties.
So, here's my advice:
if you are young, go get naked with your friends and sing.
The world sucks so sing.
It does not matter what songs,
sing them into your bodies and let them be naked and kid you not
the world will take notice
and maybe, for a little while,
it won't suck so much.

SPEAK AMERICAN

I've tried to speak American.
All my students are from America.
One is from San Paolo. One is from Oslo.
They speak beautifully American to one another in Swiss and
    Portuguese.
I tried to talk to the Dominican in Spanish but quickly realized
the only words I knew were curse words.

The most American thing I have ever said is *I love you*
but that's more international, even in space.
I slept in a sleeping bag with my 10-year-old crush
under the stars in upstate NY
and when she touched my neck I said, *Mi amore.*
I had seen Sophie Loren in *Marriage Italian Style*
and under that canopy of flickering light
believed I was a Sicilian love queen movie star.
My crush crushed my heart two weeks later in her American accent.
She said, *I don't love you. I love John Henry.*

These days I wonder if being an immigrant is the most American
    thing you can be. Saying the *immigrant* is not politically correct.
Saying the non-dominant tribe is always the tribe you don't belong
    to.
I want to belong to the *I Love You Tribe*
so I can kick all the poets in the ass and say, your next book will be
    called
The Book of Be Nice. Who wants to be nice anymore?
The lawyers don't,
and the drug store owners who used to own local drug stores
but got crushed by Walgreens. That's talking in American. Being
    crushed.
Not saying a single word.

ABOUT MATTHEW LIPPMAN

Matthew Lippman is the author of four poetry collections—*The New Year of Yellow* (winner of the Kathryn A. Morton Prize, Sarabande Books), *Monkey Bars, Salami Jew*, and *American Chew* (winner of the Burnside Review of Books Poetry Prize).

ABOUT THE POEMS

I write out of an urgency to fall into some kind of deeply quiet and contemplative state. If I am lucky enough to get there the poems which arrive are ones that deal with everyday things in the most imaginative ways that I can muster. Making a poem is also about having fun. I can dance and sing, cook and meander, fall asleep and throw a javelin, in any way that feels good. As I have gotten older I have tried to have a mix of the self and the world in the work. There is always a way in which I am trying to find links between what is deeply personal and what is not deeply personal. I like to be the falling-down-in-the-mud-hero of my poems. I want the work to be funny, tender, loving, and sometimes, a little dangerous, a little violent, a little edgy, too. It's all about getting deeper inside the great mystery.

Leslie Ullman

AS I DROVE AWAY FROM HOME

I resolved not to forget the open acres, their
never-still grasses and sage showing light
green undersides in the wind, adobe
houses hand-smoothed and in want of
sealing and new paint, the Sangre de Christo
wall of pushed-up tectonics, and Pedernale
in the distance—that mystery, that lone
perfect mesa, that monument to
Georgia O'Keeffe who also flourished
alone, towering, in thin air and strong sun—
all this, mine and not mine. My hands
have never scooped the mud that every spring
fills winter's cracks in the venerable church
of St. Francis. The people who've spoken
Spanish here for four centuries, cloistered
and simmering, would never understand
my careful, grammatical attempts, nor I
their guttural remnants of what once was
perfect Castilian. They do not meet
my eye. They count their money slowly
in Walmart's checkout line, as though today's
currency were a foreign language. And I
am a currency even more baffling, barely
tolerated, another degree of pollution in a history
long compromised and made toxic. Culpable
in my birthplace far from this land of *penitentes*
and their *moradas* so old, so earthen, so saturated
in violent and sustaining ritual, they vibrate
behind their locked gates. Yet the land, so much
itself, stretches before all of us day after day, in all shades
of light, unscrolling the gift of itself without holding back.

NOT HOLDING BACK

What is required?—a sail
full-bellied in the wind. Hand
calm at the helm. Eye trained on
a vague horizon as the harbor
shrinks behind—safe and known
and too small, suddenly, to contain
the future. The vessel's a sturdy
beetle riding the swells. Which grow.
And the depths swell beneath it,
the invisible realm of sand—restless
waves of it—and coral ridges and
caves, seaweeds, fish drifting
in clouds that hold their own light.
Such a universe—feel the vastness
and pull of it, the terrifying
power. Go with it. Let guesswork
guide you through all you can't
see. The sky goes with you.
It will answer when you ask.

WHEN YOU ASK

what will you ask first?
So many choices. And so much
you don't have, though only rarely
is there not enough. Do you remember
wanting something just because
it was a word you didn't know?
Perhaps, it was *hollyhock*.
Long ago. Now there are
words that don't
do enough. *Filibuster*
sounds solid on the tongue,
in the news, but it doesn't hold
when the self you're trying
to come to terms with resists
yet again a pattern whose precursor
is surrender. *Surrender*
has promise. But sometimes withholds
earnest money. Still looks for
the better deal, the dream house,
retribution waiting on the doorstep
and a shape-shifting fulfillment
you never, in spite of yourself,
stopped reaching for, only to
find yourself clutching air. *Fulfillment*....
It's time to outgrow a word
so empty in its clothes—maybe you meant
success. Maybe you meant
being seen. Maybe you meant...
living in another skin next time around.

NEXT TIME AROUND

I will master the pirouette and the splits
before the age of six (in this life it was
the headstand). Or learn to type
before I can write. Or climb from
my first glimpse of a river
bearing a clay jar of water on my head,
my head proud on its stalk, the water
supple, alive in its enclosure.
I might hear an ancient song rising
unbidden in my throat. Or play
a small stringed instrument while perched
in a tree. Beside the river. Singing
with the river in its own language,
having stepped without
looking back into the life
I've been given, in a country
whose small change flows through
my hands and whose ways are the air
I breathe without knowing I breathe.
I will not have to be taught to dance.
I will feel easy with beasts or, elsewhere
altogether, with the circuits inside
slender electronic devices
and the invisible chambers of the gigabyte.
For a long time I will have few
regrets, alive in that time and place
until my voice, my limbs, my thoughts
begin to reach, as though towards greater light,
towards whatever else I might have done but didn't.

WHATEVER ELSE I MIGHT HAVE DONE BUT DIDN'T

I have managed to not do harm (unless
mosquitos count, and ants when they appear
next to the canisters on my white
counter, black grains of them smaller
than rice, vaporized under the sponge
with my hand on it, and the centipede
I once found in the leg of my jeans
and the snake I mistook for a rattler
stretched across my doorway—I went
for the bladed shovel—and that
I do regret, with what has become
a residual ache of the stab, the torrent,
the *what have I done* that doubled me over)—

I *have* done harm. And now
I recall my repeated failures to walk
in the shoes of someone who
hurt me or pissed me off or lied to me.
Failures to praise, failures to listen,
failures to get in a bully's face.
Failures to pick up the phone
in a spirit of welcome. Failures to meet
the eyes of a panhandler at an intersection
even as I noted the hard beauty
of bone beneath his weathered cheek.

What will my face reveal about me
when I'm too old to rearrange it,
when I've really forgotten, when I am
no longer at my own mercy—what little of it
I tended? What shape will mercy take
then, and where will it come from?

I have done harm. It has gone around
and come around, but sometimes

it rearranged itself into lessons I could
read. In the reading, I let myself
double over and be flooded. Speared
and washed clean. In the reading, at least
for those moments, I was harmless.

HARMLESS

Most animals in populated areas
of Europe and the U.S.
Most animals who live with humans.
All animals while drinking water.
Animals while asleep.

I mean *without guile*.
Dwelling in a singularity
of focus, a state natural to them
and rare in humans. Harmless
to humans, in whom singular focus

is hard-won unless they're threatened
or hunting. Animals harm animals they hunt
but rarely hunt humans unless humans
threaten them, though in swamps
and sea water, all bets are off—

consider alligators, water moccasins, sharks,
jellyfish, lampreys flashing a single tooth,
the giant squid, the Monster of Loch Ness,
the piranha, the killer whale who wouldn't
have killed humans if humans hadn't

corralled it and broken its heart—humans
don't belong in water anyway, not
any more, their former dominion over it
several million years expired. Some animals
who thrive in water remain uncontested, cold-
blooded and totally *other*, sustaining multiple
traditions of cautionary tales, revered and feared
by those who speak and sing, grow hair, bear
burdens of memory, nurse their young,
know how to smile, and walk on two legs

that are neither swift nor strong.

ABOUT LESLIE ULLMAN

Leslie Ullman is the author of four poetry collections, most recently *Progress on the Subject of Immensity* (University of New Mexico Press, 2013. Her first collection, *Natural Histories*, won the Yale Series of Younger Poets Prize, and *Slow Work Through Sand* won the Iowa Poetry Prize. Her fifth collection, *The You That All Along Has Housed You*, will be published by Nine Mile Press in 2019. She also has published a hybrid book of craft essays and writing  exercises, *Library of Small Happiness* (3: A Taos Press, 2017), several of whose essays have appeared in *The Writer's Chronicle*. She is Professor Emerita at University of Texas-El Paso and continues to teach in the low-residency MFA Program at Vermont College of the Fine Arts. Now a resident of Taos, New Mexico, she also teaches skiing in the winters at Taos Ski Valley.

ABOUT THE POEMS

My forthcoming collection (*The You That All Along Has Housed You*, to be published by Nine Mile Press in 2019) grew from a poem-a-day experiment with writer friends. We agreed to not critique the work, to not respond unless we wished, and to not even to read the poems if pressed for time. This offered me a spaciousness I didn't expect, an arena in which self-consciousness had no purchase, and I found myself enjoying the rigors of following/nudging my own language into a compressed trajectory towards a closure I could at least accept, if not delight in—at least for the moment. The biggest difficulty was finding a subject or approach day after day on demand, which is how I ended up using the ending of the previous day's poem as the title or first line of the next poem. And I was surprised how these "given" titles catapulted me gently into unexpected directions and a greater sense of play. Of course I ended up with duds, and even with the keepers I had to comb through again and again to detect the self-indulgent touches and shortcuts which are allowable in a poem-a-day project but not in a publication.

This project also gave me a greater appreciation for seemingly "transparent" poets (to use Ron Padgett's term) like Frank O'Hara, William Stafford, and Padgett himself, whose poems appear direct and conversational but offer subtle depths and surprising trajectories. And all this, in turn, led me to explore the work of several poets, along with the processes embraced in the art world by the Abstract Expressionists, through the lens of my own experience; the result was *Press Send: Risk, Intuition, and the Transparent* Poem, available in my book of essays and the AWP archives.

NOTE: Not Holding Back appeared in *The Heart's Many Doors: American Poets Respond to Metka Krašovic's Images Responding to Emily Dickinson*, ed. by Richard Jackson, Wings Press, 2017. Next Time Around appeared in the *Journal of Feminist Studies and Religion*.

Dannye Romine Powell

LONGING REMEMBERS THE RED ROCKER INN

A place in the mountains
she and her husband visited years ago.
The woman who owned it
sat on the porch swing
and told them her son had died
at sixteen. Longing couldn't believe
how serene the woman seemed, how brave
and unscathed. Longing herself
was young then, still a brunette
and slim, her own son barely twenty
and already a drunk. Now he's made it
to forty, a miraculous feat,
though Longing's not making any bets
on the next ten. Sometimes
Longing wonders what happened
to the woman at the inn,
if she still spends evenings in the swing,
one narrow black slipper pushing against
the porch floor to keep herself going.

LONGING WEEPS AT THE BBQ SHACK IN CASHIERS, NORTH CAROLINA

She blames it on the music,
the guitarist over there
under the trees
belting out "Sunday Morning Coming Down,"
a song her son played
back in his teens. No wonder
her tears, last night's news
that he's hitting the bottle again
still salty and raw. After
all these years, Longing believes
she's grown accustomed
to this seesaw of slurred promises
and boozy refusals, believes
she can go through her days
without giving him much thought.
And usually she can – until the words
to the old songs drift by
and she remembers back to a time
when she kept his Legos
in the blue plastic tub, his toy soldiers
in the red one, and no matter his havoc,
she could pick up the pieces
and make everything look just so.

LONGING WAITS IN THE NARROW GARDEN

Pink petals strewn here
and there along the slate path
like careless thoughts.
How she used to sit in this garden,
vines and shrubs nearly obscuring
the outward view, and pretend
she lived in a distant town,
one with carousels with gold rings,
gardens complicated with mazes
and lanes lined with turreted bakeries
that had survived wars
and plagues. This was long ago,
before certain things happened,
before she could sit for hours
in the red glider in the garden
at the side of her house
and call it paradise.

ABOUT DANNYE ROMINE POWELL

Most of my life I have spent as a journalist, first as book review editor for the Charlotte (N.C.) Observer and then as a local front columnist and a few years ago, back to the book page, which was then cut from the paper two years ago. Poetry is my secret and favorite writing. I have four collections and am putting together a fifth, to be called, tentatively, "In the Sun Room with Raymond Carver." My fourth collection, "Nobody Calls Me Darling Anymore," came out in 2015 from Press 53 out of Winston-Salem, N.C. I've won fellowships from the NEA, the NC Arts Council and Yaddo, where I enjoyed living in Sylvia Plath's bedroom one cold winter several years back. I've had no formal training in poetry, though I majored in English. I have poems forthcoming in Beloit Poetry Journal and Arts & Letters and recently two appeared in The Baltimore Review. I live in Charlotte, N.C. The highlight of my week is meeting with my afternoon poetry critique group, which has been together (most of us) for more than thirty years.

ABOUT THE POEMS

I have a son who is a frequently relapsing alcoholic. There are no words outside of poetry to express the anguish of watching a beloved son destroy himself, drink by drink. These three poems are from a series of Longing poems, most of which concern this son, who, as I write this, has three months of sobriety. His pain is my pain and my pain is my muse. My hope is that the poems are sympathetic, although sometimes my anger and frustration come through. I do believe there will come a day when I can actually sit in the narrow garden of the poem and look back over my life—and his —and see the good that has come from this most stealthy of diseases and be grateful.

Markie Jo Crismon

THE CACKLE AND SHRIEK WILL KEEP YOU FROM SLEEP

The skipping sound and burning white noise
of a poor recording of the "calls of a backyard grackle"
is now in my YouTube search history. The internet is good
for these sorts of things, for filling vacancy with vacancy.

The stutter and shriek of loneliness from a bird
so often mistaken for a crow, awakens an ugliness.
"People also search for starling sounds, mockingbird sounds,
catbird sounds, meadowlark sounds, loon sounds," but no songs.

The grackle may be more elegant in shape than the crows
I love, but the song is all wrong. I want to adore this bird
like I adore the bad singers at church – always off key and so loud.
Who am I to judge? Who am I to point to its ugliness,
its loneliness, its song and say this? This. As if
the weight of this is enough to let you know all is forgiven.

ODE TO MY MESSY BUN

It's become a joke, the women
who keep secrets in their hair.
But, where else do you hide such things?

It's so stupid, the creation of a nest
on purpose, partly because
I can't stand the feeling of hair

smothering my neck, partly
to show off my hidden shave because,
also stupid, I feel like a badass.

The nest is brown, with a streak
of gold to let strangers know
this nest is different.

The nest seems to balance on the head,
but it is held taught with hidden pins
to hide the effort of its construction.

The nest has been stretched and twisted
in ways that seem unkind to the natural
fibers that are still so connected to my scalp.

This is not a nest for baby birds or children
to leave behind to build more nests. This nest
is made to fill emptiness, while appearing empty.

T and F always hate when I cut my hair
short. *Long locks are for the desirable woman.*
I am not used to being a desirable woman.

I am learning to feel good
about my mind, my body.
I go to therapy. I buy clothes that fit.

I talk to D once a week (going on three years now).
We argue sometimes, but I mostly feel
better. I feel good crying on that couch.

There is something about a mess on purpose.
There is something about a nest on purpose.

MAN FOR WOMAN - FRIDGE

I keep my washed grapes in a bowl
in the refrigerator, just like you did.
I like thinking of things from back then.

When time dripped from all the faucets
and we should have but didn't even bother
to tell the landlord or fix it ourselves.

We were young and in our prime,
but still awkward in our bodies. You
lumbering around looking for trousers.

Me wading through waves of sleep. I fumble
through question words. You mutter something:
a walk, fresh air, can't sleep. clown will eat me.

No one laughs and we are in two different
landscapes. Wrapped in fresh linens,
because I felt good enough to do laundry,

I bury myself in pillows, like a child seeing
if she can stop breathing long enough
to disappear from her mother walking by.

Even then, I was old enough to know love can't
change the trajectory of a torpedo or an air bomb.
The child in me waves her arms, longing.

To be held up by a panting, battered body that wants
to knock you out cold, but exhaustion keeps you
together sweaty, bruised and bleeding, is still love.

I needed more than the fear of becoming the woman
in your refrigerator. Wrinkled grapes; not yet raisins,
if it weren't for the texture, we could enjoy the sweetness.

ABOUT MARKIE JO CRISMON

Markie Jo Crismon's therapist often compares her to an orchid. Depending on the day, Markie Jo takes this to mean that she has dressed loudly, is some sort of fragrant, is fragile, was purchased at a Trader Joes' on a whim, or when she's feeling particularly macabre – easy to kill. What her therapist is trying to say is that she has very specific needs when it comes to care, self or otherwise. She prefers to think of herself as particular.

Markie Jo started collecting antiques sometime in grade school and used to have a small bucket of sharp metal objects that she found on the ground. It is a miracle she never contracted tetanus. She likes crosswords and baseball and used to make short films. After several months, she realized her puppy Winslow is really a Kevin, but it's too late. Markie Jo has a difficult time writing bios about herself because she has not published a book or traveled the world, but she would like to do these things.

She received her Bachelor of Arts in Creative Writing from Knox College and is currently working toward a Master of Fine Arts in Poetry at University of Missouri-St. Louis.

ABOUT THE POEMS

The poems attempt to explore distance—from ourselves and others—and how we interact with that space and time. Cup it in our hands, stretch it, set it on fire. The disconnect created by this distance, or perhaps vice versa, in these poems suggests that the things in arm's reach are the most damaging, but there is always a glimmer of hope and forgiveness.

These poems also quietly ask how pop culture and the internet add to this distance and disconnect. Rather than sit with our loneliness, we immerse ourselves in information and televised distractions curating a marketable personhood to consume the one we fear is not presentable enough to wear out of the house. But sifting through this loss and fear reveals an opening into who we are and what guides us and the power to reach out and reclaim it.

Canto III: The Significance of a Memory
Ezra Pound Finds A Style & Form

1.

It is April, 1908. Ezra Pound has just arrived in Venice. There is some scandal behind him: He was asked to resign two months ago from Wabash College in Crawfordsville, Indiana, after his landladies discovered a girl in his bed, whereupon they informed the college president and at least two of the trustees. Pound's defense was that he'd slept in his office, not in his rented rooms, because he'd discovered the poor woman, a chorus girl, stranded in a snowstorm without shelter or transportation, and to help her out, he'd given her his bed; but few seemed willing to grant the story or him much credence. In their view, his behavior has been deliberately provocative since the day he arrived here a year ago, to become Chair and sole faculty member of its newly-formed Department of Romance Languages. There have been reports of him smoking, drinking, staying up all hours, entertaining women, and the college has been looking to rid itself of him, in which effort the landladies' report has proved extremely useful. After some back and forth, Pound agreed to depart, with a small severance. No one was sorry to see him go, least of all Pound himself, who left not only this position and, as it turned out, this kind of academic career, but also a town and a state which he labeled "the sixth circle of hell" (the one where the heretics burn constantly, being so far from heaven). Now, finally, he had thought, he could begin his life's real calling, as a poet and a maker of culture.

He sailed from New York to Gibraltar, lingering a few weeks to augment his meagre funds with a job earning $15 a day as a tour guide for Americans. Now has come to Venice, renting a room over a bakery near the San Vio bridge. It is a short half-mile walk to the Dogana, the old custom house, and he takes it sometimes to look across the Grand Canal to Saint Mark's Square. He is poor, having only the diminished remains of his severance from the college and his Gibraltar earnings, and so cannot afford a gondola to cross the canal to mingle with the crowds and see the sights up close. This moment of gazing and longing will stay with him as a significant memory. A dozen years hence it will serve as a turning point as he develops his epic poem, *The Cantos*.

For now, the important things are that he has begun his full-time vocation, and that he has a plan. He has written poems before, of course, but this break gives him the opportunity to embark on his new career as a full-time writer. On July 20, three months after arrival, he publishes *A Lume Spento,* his first book. It comes in green wrappers under the name of publisher A. Antonini; but it is in fact a private printing, financed by Pound. This fact hardly deters him, for whatever else it is, it is a beginning, and treated right, it can show momentum gathering to him, and bring him some attention. By early August he has moved from Venice to London, where he persuades prominent bookseller and publisher Elkin Mathews to display the book in his bookshop, an influential London literary venue. In another good development, the *London Evening Standard* calls the book "wild and haunting stuff, absolutely poetic, original, imaginative, passionate, and spiritual," though it is possible that the review is a blind written by Pound himself. In any case, he pushes the book hard, by every means at hand. This is his life now, and he must make it a success; as he writes to his father, "no vulgarity of publicity need be shunned..."

He believes that London is the only place in which to launch his new career if he is to have the best chance at success, for London in 1908 is the Rome of its day, one of the world's great cultural and economic centers. More important for him, it is also the center of the poetry universe. He can accomplish more there in a year, he says, than he could in ten years in America. He sets to it, working hard, living on a meagre four pounds per month—about $20—sent him by his father, doing his daily work at the British Museum Reading Room. Though he is invited to some dinners and literary gatherings, he is an outsider, this American from the provinces, all energy and animation, an often irritating contrast to the other more staid attendees, whom he seems to offend almost as much as he sometimes charms.

But nothing stops him, or at least, he is determined to let nothing stop him. Late that year he gathers poems from the handwritten manuscript which academics now call *The San Trovaso*

Notebook for a second collection, titling it *A Quinzaine For This Yule.*
It is published in December, one hundred copies under the name of
publisher Pollock and Co. It is is initially another self-financed
venture, until Elkin Mathews agrees to finance an additional one
hundred copies. In the new year, January, 1909, he launches a
lecture series on literature in southern Europe. The audience is
small, only 55 people, and so brings only a small financial return;
but the advertisements go everywhere, a surge of publicity that
introduces him as—a poet. This is good marketing. It's the
recognition he wants. It increases his momentum and visibility, and
Mathews agrees to publish a new collection of his work, *Personae of
Ezra Pound,* to come out in April, with half the poems taken from *A
Lume Spento,* and the other half to be new. This is another
validation, for Mathews is a reputable publisher of poetry, printing
thirty to forty elegant volumes per year, from a list that includes
such "names" as Lionel Johnson, Ernest Dowson, Fiona Macleod,
and W. B. Yeats. The new book is widely reviewed and in general,
it is highly praised, though there are notes of caution. Reviewers
sense that something new is taking place, and that it offers a
powerful disturbance of the established order. They like what they
see, but they are unsure about what this new thing is or where it is
going.

Pound is still a young man, only 23 years old, but he is
beginning to have a name. He makes the most of his new persona
as *artiste* and poet, for this is his moment, he is *being noticed.* His
appearance, for example, always somewhat eccentric, now takes a
wilder turn. Ford Maddox Ford gives a description of an encounter
with Pound:

> Ezra ... would approach with the step of a dancer, making
> passes with a cane at an imaginary opponent. He would wear
> trousers made of green billiard cloth, a pink coat, a blue shirt, a
> tie hand-painted by a Japanese friend, an immense sombrero, a
> flaming beard cut to a point, and a single, large blue earring.

This matter of appearance is not frivolous. It is the outward
show of the masks he adopts and is integral to his work. Persona

and work are related, in his view, for he sees the persona as the finder of fact, the creator of the made work. As the persona changes so does the work. Assaying the early poems and the first thirty Cantos, the critic R.P. Blackmur will describe this relation in an influential 1933 essay, "The Masks of Ezra Pound": "Mr. Pound's work has been to make *personae*, to become himself, as a poet, in this special sense a person through which what has most interested him in life and letters might be given voice."

The changes that these masks engender—in voice, range, and subject matter—are easy enough to see by sampling random pages in successive volumes. For example, there is tremendous distance from the archaism of "Sharing his exile that hath borne the flame" of *A Lume Spento* (1908), to "The jewelled steps are already quite white with dew, / It is so late that the dew soaks my gauze stockings," from *Cathay* (1915), to the cold ironic voice of "The little Millwins attend the Russian Ballet. / The mauve and greenish souls of the little Millwins / Were seen lying along the upper seats / Like so many unused boas" of *Lustra* (1917), to the heady rhetoric of "And then went down to the ship, / Set keel to breakers, forth on the godly sea, and / We set up mast and sail on that swart ship," from "Canto I." Truly, if you did not see the author's name on the individual books, you would think that they were written by different poets—which, in a way, they were.

2.

More changes are taking place, very rapidly, as Pound in this apprenticeship is inventing what it means to be a modernist, creating such new movements and books as Imagism and Vorticism, and *Cathay*, *Blast*, and *Personae*, and through associations with such powerful creative artists as Yeats, Henri Gaudier-Brzeska, Wyndham Lewis, T.E. Hulme, H.D., T.S. Eliot, and James Joyce. In these years of rapid intellectual and aesthetic movement, he has begun publishing at least one and often two books a year, and will do so for most of the rest of his life. In these years of fast motion, everything he touches changes him, and he in turn changes everything he touches.

He studies hard, gleaning everything he can from his chosen masters, of whom four are especially important at this time: Yeats, for whom he acts as secretary in 1913-1914; Ford Maddox Hueffer (later Ford), editor of the *English Review*, whom during his afternoon visits in 1909 and 1910 jars Pound out of his use of archaic and stilted language by rolling on the floor with laughter after reading some of it; Guido Calvacanti (1250-1300), friend to Dante Alighieri, whose work Pound begins translating and praising in 1910, and who remains a lifelong influence; and Robert Browning (1812-1889), the great Victorian poet, in some ways the most influential and useful of these masters as Pound tries to move forward from his early work. Browning has overcome many of the challenges that Pound faces as he moves to meet his next goal, writing a long poem, an ambition he has spoken of since even before 1905, when he was an undergraduate preparing for his BA from Hamilton College.

His major makeshift lesson-plan is *Sordello*, Browning's 5,982 line poem in rhymed couplets. Pound considers it the last great epic poem in English. He also reads deeply in another Browning major work, *The Ring and the Book*. From these he learns how to structure a long poem, and how to expand the field of the poem to bring reality into it. He learns something else that will affect his poetry for the rest of his life: that the teller of tales must ground his tales in fact. Browning did this by using *The Yellow Book* for *The Ring and the Book*, and used descriptions of actual scenes of Venice for *Sordello*. Browning's example also teaches him about the use of a subjective paratactic narration that will ground his style as he begins his first drafts in 1915 in what will become *The Cantos*.

For this beginning of his own long poem he returns in memory to that brief sojourn in Venice, publishing a rambling set of three Cantos in three successive issues of *Poetry Magazine,* which gives him the headline position in its June 1917 issue. The three poems showcase both his entanglement and his frustration with his literary father from their opening line: "Hang it all, there can be but one *Sordello*!"—an icebreaker if ever there was one. Indeed, Browning's influence has become so dominant, that Pound will have to be confront and discard him before he can truly begin his life's major work on *The Cantos*.

He is not satisfied by these first efforts. The Browning influence is part of the reason, but there is more. He knows this is to be a long poem, but he doesn't have the style or range for it yet.

Making the point by activity, Pound immediately starts revising these ur-Cantos, sharpening the images, tightening some lines and dropping many others, seeking economy, compression, and speed. In October he publishes the poems in a slightly revised form in *Lustra* (New York: Alfred A. Knopf, 1917) as "Three Cantos of a Poem of Some Length," and in February through April, 1918, he publishes further revisions in a London periodical *The Future*. He is working hard at them, but he knows that the changes are not enough, that they have to change more, but he does not know how to do it yet. He believes that he is near to finding the right style, but he senses that he has not yet grasped the full extent of the lessons from his chosen masters or the breadth of the challenge before him. He writes Cantos IV-VII, publishing them in *The Dial* in 1921, using a voice and temperament similar to the first three, but he finds these still unsatisfactory. As he writes his father in December 1919, "done cantos 5,6,7, each more incomprehensible than the one preceding it."

3.

It will take his experience of three large changes to gain the knowledge needed to bring these early ur-Cantos to their current form, though to say it that way is to falsify the process, for makes it sound as if the creativity involved in these changes was direct, a movement from "a" to "b" to "c." Hardly. Nothing comes whole to his mind; there is no sudden flash. It is instead a series of incremental changes and discoveries. His his openness to everything in the cultural air around him helps him gain this exposure, and his driving ambition and artistic honesty keep him from accepting imperfect settlements. Ultimately he will drop much of what he has written and embark instead on something completely different for him and completely new in poetry.

The first of these experiences is his exposure to new work by James Joyce and T.S. Eliot in 1918 and 1919. The second is his own new work in poetry and criticism between 1918 and 1921, and the third is his work with Chinese poetry and language in this same period.

His exposure to *Ulysses* comes because he has helped to get the book published in serial form in *The Little Magazine* starting in 1918. Reading the proofs, he is fascinated by Joyce's technique of combining different styles, high and low, his methods of increasing the speed of narration and the numbers of voices, of bringing humor into serious work, systematically using allusive fragments or narrative, while at the same time developing memorable characters. He finds the combination of all this wonderful and brilliant, but doesn't at first see how these techniques can be used in poetry, until he sees what Eliot does with them in *Gerontion* (1919) and then later in *The Waste Land,* which Pound helps edit. This does not cause an immediate change in his work or thought, but it is suggestive, something to think about.

In these years he writes two longish and breathtakingly brilliant pieces, "Homage to Sextus Propertius" in 1919, and "Hugh Selwyn Mauberley" in 1920, both extending his idea of what a poem can do. He is refining his craft, work by work, redefining the field of the poem and its relation to history and historical persons. He is also writing a great deal of criticism, more than at any other time in his life: at least 13 pieces every year between 1912 and 1921, and in 1918, a staggering 102 articles. Like the poetry, these articles often seek to re-think the aims and craft of the art, like the *Imagiste Manifesto*, written in 1911 and published in 1913, which is the same year in which he receives the notes that will become a foundational piece he prints in 1919 as "The Chinese Written Character as a Medium for Poetry." This essay is in fact a misreading of the real nature of Chinese characters, a blemish that he apparently never discovers; but its inaccuracy does not affect its usefulness to him. It suggests a way for him to make elements he believes basic to Chinese characters a form for his poetry. He calls this an ideogrammatic method, and it is radical. Two decades later he will describe the technique this way, in *Guide to Kulchur* (1938):

> The ideogrammatic method consists of presenting one factor and then another until at some point one gets off the dead and desensitized surface of the reader's mind, onto a part that will register.

This combination of examples—the modernist techniques of Joyce and Eliot, the ancient language techniques and ideograms of the Chinese, and techniques of narration and development that he has worked into his poetry—come together in the summer of 1919 as he works on Canto IV. He is writing the poetry as if it were an ideogram, in a compressed style with many voices and episodes. He collocates items and episodes that run from Troy and Homer, to Ovid, medieval Provence, China and Japan within the broad theme of the terrible results of men's exploitation of women and of the energies of nature, and their opposition, the delight in living in accord with these forces rather than seeking to control or to posses them.

It is a new aesthetic, the breakthrough he has sought. Pound feels free to bring in any episodes that reveal underlying relations, without any necessity to state or define those relations. Thus the canto opens with "Palace in smoky light, / Troy but a heap of smoldering boundary stones," referring to a city destroyed, and then moves quickly to the first story, a horrible one of Procne avenging her husband's rape of her sister by killing and boiling their son, and serving the cooked child to the father. More such stories follow. Interspersed are beautiful descriptions—"The liquid and rushing crystal / beneath the knees of the gods. / Ply over ply, thin glitter of water" or "Dawn, to our waking, drifts in the green cool light; / Dew-haze blurs, in the grass, pale ankles moving." Through it all there is no argument, no narration, no plot, no single character or authorial point of view, no traditional way for a reader to find moral or intellectual bearings. There has never been a poetry like this in English. Everything is *present*, everything is connected. The world presented is flat, nonhierarchical, and the only meaning is to be found in the relations created by the reader as he or she experiences the work presented. It is, in a way, a complete intellectual an aesthetic liberation, a true disruption: For the individual intellect is liberated from all authority, including the authority of narrative, history, and culture, and is set free to find its own relations between the materials.

This is the first key change, the invention of a new style. It has taken him four years from the start of writing the first ur-cantos to reach this moment in 1919. He makes one more change, this one in tone, bringing irony and humor to Canto VIII, which he finishes in January, 1922. This is the second major change, and it completes his development of the style of the cantos.

Writing this Canto helps him refine his form. As it develops it seems to repeat the divine epiphany of ur-Canto I, but in this newer more compressed style. He doesn't need both, and so he replaces the old ur-Canto II with the new Canto VIII. In this restructuring the Browning influence is reduced to just a few lines: "Hang it all, Robert Browning, / there can be but the one "Sordello." / But Sordello, and my Sordello?" So they begin, not gently, not obeisance to a master, but as a revolt, a direct assault, ferocious and assured. The changes are not done. The new style and form continue to show him ways to restructure the older work. Within the year he drops and rewrites major parts of the old Canto III, and then moves the rewrite to become Canto I of his poem, which now begins, "And then went down to the ship."

This conversion from the old form of the poem to the new one is now almost done. With one more change the ur-Cantos will no longer part of his opening sequence, and Browning's influence will be done with, only the skills learned from him remaining. Pound's work on the new Canto III is the third big change, bringing the style and method of the long poem into focus, and as part of that, making the 1908 events from his own life integral to the the claim that this poem is an epic and a celebration of himself as its author.

4.

It is 1923 as he writes the new Canto III, fifteen years since the moment of looking across the Venetian canal. The new work begins its development as a rewrite from the old. The framework he needs is partly there in the old ur-Cantos, but it is in the old style, and it lacks the new compression:

> Your "palace step"?
> My stone seat was the Dogana's curb,
> And there were not "those girls," there was one flare, one face.
> 'Twas all I ever saw, but it was real….

And I can no more say what shape it was ...
But she was young, too young.

These lines were a response to a passage from Browning's
poem, in which the character Sordello takes inventory and makes
judgment on his life and the life in the city around him:

I muse this on a ruined palace-step
At Venice: why should I break off, nor sit
Longer upon my step, exhaust the fit
England gave birth to? Who 's adorable
Enough reclaim a——no Sordello's Will
Alack!—be queen to me? That Bassanese
Busied among her smoking fruit-boats? These
Perhaps from our delicious Asolo
Who twinkle, pigeons o'er the portico
Not prettier, bind June lilies into sheaves
To deck the bridge-side chapel, dropping leaves
Because it is pleasant to be young,
Soiled by their own loose gold-meal?
   Ah, beneath
The cool arch stoops she, brownest cheek! Her wreath
Endures a month—a half month—if I make
A queen of her, continue for her sake
Sordello's story? Nay, that Paduan girl
Splashes with barer legs where a live whirl
In the dead black Giudecca proves sea-weed
Drifting has sucked down three, four, all indeed
Save one pale-red striped, pale-blue turbaned post
For gondolas.
   You sad dishevelled ghost
That pluck at me and point, are you advised
I breathe? Let stay those girls (e'en her disguised
—Jewels i' the locks that love no crownet like
Their native field-buds and the green wheat-spike,
So fair!—who left this end of June's turmoil,
Shook off, as might a lily its gold soil,

Pomp, save a foolish gem or two, and free
In dream, came join the peasants o'er the sea).
Look they too happy, too tricked out? Confess
There is such niggard stock of happiness
To share, that, do one's uttermost, dear wretch,
One labors ineffectually to stretch…

Pound's chiding about his place on the "curb" versus the "ruined palace step" of the other is part of the ur-Canto methods of querying and responding to Browning's poem. Dialogue and argument with the other poem about facts and values occupied much of the writing in those older first efforts, a struggle that betrayed a deep anxiety of influence, for as much as Pound admired Browning, even in that early stage he did not want to be overwhelmed by him. He knew that he was accumulating significant debts to the other, from this study of *Sordello,* and his reading in *The Ring and the Book.* Some more theoretical debt may have come from reading Browning's discussion about poetry and history in an 1852 introductory essay to *Letters of Percy Bysshe Shelley,* that argued that poetry can organize and validate the jumble of facts that history would otherwise would be, and make it into something more permanent and freighted with universal truths:

> There is a time when the general eye has, so to speak,
> absorbed its fill of the phenomena around it, whether spiritual
> or material, and desires rather to learn the exacter significance
> of what it possesses, than to receive any augmentation of what
> is possessed. Then is the opportunity for the poet of loftier
> vision, to lift his fellows, with their half-apprehensions, up to
> his own sphere, by intensifying the import of details and
> rounding the universal meaning.

What Pound drew from that, and from the essay's discussion of the two kinds of poets (objective and subjective), as well as from *Sordello,* where he saw the theory in practice, is that the great poetic chore was neither factual accuracy on the one hand nor imaginative self-expression on the other, but historic truth as created by the deep working of the poetic imagination. (There are ironies here: The letters turned out to be spurious, a claim for something that should have existed, but did not, and the book was quickly recalled and suppressed. But for those who saw it, Browning's essay was not well-received: "We are bound to state that the conceit of much of Mr. Browning's introductory discourse is equalled only by its very indifferent English and most questionable grammar; and that the conceit, the bad English, and the careless grammar, are all surpassed by the pervading obscurity of style and thought, which to the ordinary reader cannot but prove distressingly tantalizing." This was *The Literary Gazette*, February 21, 1852, a review apparently written before the fraud was exposed.)

Beyond these philosophical and methodological inheritances from the other poet there was another area where the debt was so large as to be potentially overwhelming if not dealt with. Pound wanted *The Cantos* to be a complimentary successor to *Sordello*, which he considered the last great epic in poetry. He knew, even as he began his "poem of some length," that it would be an epic. The problem he faced was how to do this, how to learn so much from a great master, and yet have it come out his own way and in his own voice. He had to create a distance, to engage and find a way around the other poet. Thus:

> Hang it all, there can be but one *Sordello*!
> But say I want to, say I take your whole bag of tricks,
> Let in your quirks and tweeks, and say the thing's an art-form,
> Your *Sordello*, and that the modern world
> Needs such a rag-bag to stuff all its thought in;
> Say that I dump my catch, shiny and silvery
> As fresh sardines flapping and slipping on the marginal
> cobbles?
> (I stand before the booth, the speech; but the truth
> Is inside this discourse—this booth is full of the marrow of
> wisdom.)
> Give up th' intaglio method....

He knew—he could not have not known—that there were problems in the technique of *Sordello*. Its convoluted rhetoric and intentional obscurity make it a difficult poem to read even by a trained reader. At the time of its publication, Alfred Lord Tennyson is reputed to have said that "There were only two lines in

it that I understood, and they were both lies; they were the opening
and closing lines, 'Who will may hear Sordello's story told,' and
'Who would has heard Sordello's story told!'" And for all that,
Pound still had to find a way around *Sordello* and this poet, this
"Bob Browning," as he called him, without letting go of it or the
questions the poet and his poem raised for his work:

> Peire Cardinal
> Was half forerunner of Dante. Arnaut's that trick
> Of the unfinished address,
> And half your dates are out, you mix your eras;
> For that great font Sordello sat beside—
> Tis an immortal passage, but the font?—
> Is some two centuries outside the picture.
> Does it matter?
>   Not in the least. Ghosts move about me
> Patched with histories. You had your business:
> To set out so much thought, so much emotion;
> To paint, more real than any dead Sordello,
> The half or third of your intensest life
> And call that third Sordello;
> And you'll say, "No, not your life,
> He never showed himself."
> Is't worth the evasion, what were the use
> Of setting figures up and breathing life upon them,
> Were 't not our life, your life, my life, extended?
> I walk Verona. (I am here in England.)
> I see Can Grande. (Can see whom you will.)
>   You had one whole man?
> And I have many fragments, less worth? Less worth?
> Ah, had you quite my age, quite such a beastly and
> cantankerous age?
> You had some basis, had some set belief.
> Am I let preach? Has it a place in music?

And so, from this quarrel, without giving up "th' intaglio
method," Pound's first writing of "My stone seat was the Dogana's

curb" is changed to the simple and more descriptive "I sat on the Dogana's steps / For the gondolas cost too much, that year" and "And there were not 'those girls,' there was one flare, one face. / 'Twas all I ever saw, but it was real...." becomes "And there were not 'those girls', there was one face"; much of that long original passage from 1917 being redrafted to a mere six lines tells us all we need to know about Pound's changed view of Browning, from being a model of technique to imitate to being a poet from whom he must depart. Pound left with his arms full, though it is interesting and even odd that Pound should have drawn so many lessons from one of the most maligned and nearly impenetrable of Browning's works. Perhaps in its obscurity and fragmentary approach to the telling of the tale, the original proved not only suggestive to Pound's creative instincts, it also gave him an aesthetic license to free himself from his other styles and personae.

5.

The rewrite of Canto III takes place in 1923, looking back at his time in Venice in 1908. He remembers sitting alone on the steps of the Venice custom house looking across the Grand Canal to Saint Mark's square, too poor to travel there by gondola. He recalls the face of a particular woman, and the sights and sounds of that moment of seeing, the members of the Buccentoro rowing club singing verses of a then-popular but vulgar song, "The Spanish Girl," the lights of the Morosini palace, and the Palazzo dei Leoni rookery on the Grand Canal:

> I sat on the Dogana's steps
> For the gondolas cost too much, that year,
> And there were not "those girls", there was one face,
> And the Buccentoro twenty yards off, howling, "Stretti",
> And the lit cross-beams, that year, in the Morosini,
> And peacocks in Koré's house, or there may have been.

These lines, with their subtle internal rhymes and the flow and echo of the vowels, are now the first personal intrusion by Pound in the poem. The poem has been eight years in development for these lines to come forth in this form. They introduce him as poet-hero, but as a passive one, sitting and observing, somewhat defeated by his lack of material resource.

It is jarring to come to these lines after the wide-ranging cultural raves through other legends, poetries, myths, and centuries, of the two predecessor Cantos. These lines almost feel random; yet for Pound, as the mini-history traced at the opening of this essay shows, these lines in fact describe something epic: For 1908 was the year in which he became a poet, published a first book, then a second, and began to make his reputation and career as a poet. In this moment of memory he makes himself part of that reality which the rest of the poem will set out to engage and contain. These personal lines telescope concerns of the rest of the poem—they are a meeting-ground of economics, finances, art, gods, history, time, and memory —and then they break off in what appears to be an inexplicable jump, this time to a god-infested vision that takes place in the present. This is also a surprise. It seems inexplicable because there is no obvious trigger, nothing to spark the vision; it appears to happen almost randomly, causelessly, and a reader is left with the sense that anything else could have happened as easily as this movement from the memory of peacocks to a current vision of gods in azure air, or from a 15-year old reverie to a current vision of gods and swimmers:

> Gods float in the azure air,
> Bright gods and Tuscan, back before dew was shed.
> Light: and the first light, before ever dew was fallen.
> Panisks, and from the oak, dryas,
> And from the apple, mælid,
> Through all the wood, and the leaves are full of voices,
> A-whisper, and the clouds bowe over the lake,
> And there are gods upon them,
> And in the water, the almond-white swimmers,
> The silvery water glazes the upturned nipple,
>   As Poggio has remarked.
> Green veins in the turquoise,
> Or, the gray steps lead up under the cedars.

But this is not random. The shift from past to present, from the deep poverty of those older days to visions of divinity of these current ones, must be viewed in the context of the making of his poetic career, from the start to realization, from poverty and joblessness to the beginning of the epic poem that will occupy the rest of his life. These opening personal lines of Canto III are the great pivot, the moment when the poem changes over, from introduction of themes and elevation of goals, aims, and achievement by reference of the first two cantos, to something both more grandiose and more specific: The announcement that this "poem of some length" will be the epic that continues the other older epics, and they are also the assertion of his vision. It is an announcement welcomed by the gods. This memory is the centerpiece of it all, the moment of reality from which the poem makes its claim for epic equivalence.

6.

Everything Pound originally wrote had to be re-framed as the style and the vision developed. He started with the change in the introductory materials. Canto I now begins "And then…" not as a new beginning but a continuation of an old story, begun before this poem was written or conceived, an addition to the reality of the world of things and acts: "And then went down to the ship," the poem begins, that "And then" announcing that this work, these acts about to take place, come after some preceding act or acts, some movement or moment undescribed here, *because not necessary to be described.* Because what comes before that line is all the rest of writing and all the rest of the world: That two-word opener is a phrase without limits, uncircumscribed, unbounded. Everything happened before this moment, and this work, this act, this moment of Pound's poem continues all of that other time and existence, all of that life.

Canto I rewrites Book XI of the *Odyssey*, Odysseus' journey to the land of the dead, in Seafarer rhythms, a tour de force conjoining of past epics, a double reference to properly set the stage in which his newly subtitled "Poem of some Length" can join their august company. Canto II then follows this at gallop with a modern language questioning of the dead as it moves through Ovid's *Metamorphoses*, Browning's *Sordello*, Euripides, Dionysus, and others, all of it conducted against a smoky postwar WWI background. Pound regarded the method of these first two cantos as parallel to the Greek rite of *nekyia*, or the questioning of the dead about the future, and thought the *nekyia* of the *Odyssey* a poem much older than the *Odyssey* itself. In the *Odyssey* original, Odysseus journeys to the Halls of Hades, across the River of Ocean to consult Tiresias. The shades of the dead gather to drink blood and speak with him, and he speaks with many of them, including with his dead mother. Tiresias tells him that he alone will survive the voyage home.

Canto II ends "And…" as the bookend to the poem's beginning "And then…" The two phrases or words frame the introduction to the work, telling us that this is an epic, and that it has a hero, and—and—that new things will take place. Pound created something new for this poem, a new style and a collage technique in which narrative is abandoned, its logical and calendar flow and unity disrupted and made plastic in favor of a method of organization that is thematic, not specific, and organic and intuitive rather than chronological or sequential in the ordinary sense of those terms. Everything taken up in the poem is before us at all times, because everything *can be* before us at all times.

The poetry of Canto III's opening is the result of his successful struggle with Browning as a literary father and master. W.B. Yeats said, "Out of the quarrel with others we make rhetoric; out of the quarrel with ourselves we make poetry." Pound's quarrel with himself, with his materials, with Robert Browning, results in this incredibly compressed and beautiful moment of reality that launches and defines The Cantos.

This new work will not appear in book form until 1925, under the title, *A draft of XVI Cantos of Ezra Pound : for the beginning of a poem of some length.* He has no idea at his time how long the poem will be, but he is sure that he is on to something, and that it is big, a poem containing history, in a new inclusive style, an epic. In 1928 he publishes *A Draft of the Cantos 17–27*, but *A Draft of XXX Cantos will not appear until 1930*, with the Hours Press, a Paris publishing house run by upper-class Brit writer, heiress, and political and civil rights activist Nancy Cunard. This will be the first chance an interested reader will have to see these poems together, the first time he or she can get a substantial sense of what the poet has been up to in this decade of intense writing.

Many found it confusing, or praised one part and ignored the rest. Louis Zukofsky and William Carlos Williams praise the work and defend it whole, as a necessary effort to open up the closed mind of western culture. W.B. Yeats, on the other hand, said that the work had "more style than form," and Eliot was harsh: "I am seldom interested in what he is saying, but only in the way he says it." Wyndham Lewis leaped over the work to judge the author, calling Pound "a revolutionary simpleton,… an intellectual eunuch." Though Pound retained good relations with them all, he stepped back a little from them, and focused more and more of his energies and advice on younger writers, urging them to do what he had done, to create their own movements and their own forms.

7.

Finally, here are some definitions that may be helpful:

Dogana is the Venice Custom House, which has striking views across the Grand Canal to buildings surrounding Saint Mark's Square.

Buccentoro means "Golden Bark," and is a rowing club situated around the corner from the Dogana.

Stretti is from a Neopolitan song that was popular then. It means "close embrace." The song is La spagnuola or The Spanish Girl. The kline is "Stretti stretti / nell'ecstasi d'amor / La spagnuola sa amar cost / bocca a bocca la notte e il di": In close embrace, in close embrace / in love's ecstasy / the Spanish girl is that way when in love / mouth to mouth, night and day.

Morosini is an aristocratic Venetian family and the name of a square and a palace.

Kore's house refers to the neglected grounds of the Palazzo dei Leoni, which had become a rookery.

Panisks are little woodland Pans.

dryas are oak tree nymphs that die when the tree dies.

maelid is a nymph of the apple trees.

Poggio is Gian Francesco Poggio Bracciolini (1380 1459), best known simply as Poggio Bracciolini, an Italian scholar and early humanist. He discovered and recovered many classical Latin manuscripts, mostly decaying and forgotten in German, Swiss, and French monastic libraries. His most celebrated find was *De rerum natura*, the only surviving work by Lucretius. The "remark" is a distortion of his description from a letter to Niccolò de' Niccoli, another humanist, about a scene he witnessed at the baths in Baden, Switzerland, in 1416.

8.

My debts for this piece are numerous. Some wonderful critics have written on these passages and on Pound. Here are the ones that were most helpful to me:

The Pound Era, Hugh Kenner, University of California Press (September 18, 1973). One of the great books on Pound and the modernists.

The Genesis of Ezra Pound's Cantos, Ronald Bush, Princeton University Press (July 14, 2014). One of the truly helpful books on The Cantos by a knowledgable critic.

Language as Gesture, R.P. Blackmur, Columbia University Press (1981) the essay on Ezra Pound titled "The Masks of Ezra Pound."

Blogging Pound's The Cantos: Canto III, Gord Sellar, Part 5 of 51, online at https://www.gordsellar.com/2012/03/06/blogging-pounds-the-cantos-canto-iii/

A Companion to The Cantos of Ezra Pound, Carroll F. Terrell, University of California Press; F Second Printing Used edition (April 16, 1993)

Ezra Pound: Poet, A Portrait of the Man and His Work, A. David Moody, Oxford University press, 2007

Ezra Pound: Poet, A Portrait of the Man and His Work, II The Epic Years, 1921-1939, A. David Moody, Oxford University press, 2014. These two volumes are terrific, indispensable for understanding the life and work.

—Bob Herz

Anne Hosansky

VISITOR

A stranger wearing the face of my daughter
Sits across her "space" from me.
The clock ticks my search for words
That won't fold her up like a prayer plant.
" I made pecan pie. "
                    "I don't eat sweets anymore."

Her jeans are ragged. Ragged, too, the shorn hair
I used to braid. A rebellious curl still Insistent
On her forehead.   One eyebrow pierced by an
Earring? God of parents, keep me silent.
"New shirt?"
                    "From someone's mother."

The kettle screams. Escaping I fetch tea
In china meant for guests. Her miniature tea set
Decaying in the attic with the dolls she served.
(I have dreamed I am an attic refugee.)
"Cream or lemon?"
                    "Plain, Daddy's way."

She's come for her books, she said,
Alice in her eternal Wonderland
When I held her on my lap reading
To the rhythm of her laughing ,"More!"
"Anything else . . . ?"
                    "Nothing."

I stir the embers in the grate. Remember,
I want to ask, the time I saw eyes staring
Through the flames? "A spirit is dying there," I said.
"I see it too," she cried, hand linked in mine.
"Remember when . . . ?"

"'I'm tired."

How like my child's her profile is.
I dream my hand across our space to touch her cheek.
She sees my hand a fisherman's net.

"I have to leave now."

I'm the one who taught her never talk to strangers.

ABOUT ANNE HOSANSKY

Anne Hosansky is making her second appearance in Nine Mile.
Her poems have also been published in *Mobius, First Literary Review
East* and *Poetica*. She was the first-place
winner of a New York Poetry Forum
contest and won a "Highly Esteemed"
citation in an Israeli publication. A prolific
prose writer, as well, she's the author of
five books, including the acclaimed
memoir *Widow's Walk*. Her short stories
and articles have been published in the
US, Canada and England. In her "other
life" she was an actor.

ABOUT THE POEM

"Visitor" is one of the most
emotionally difficult poems I've ever written. Originally the
rejoinders by the daughter weren't there, only the mother's words
and thoughts. But the poem felt one-sided . I don't know where the
idea of letting the daughter speak came from. Maybe my Muse
decided to lend a wing (as she often has to!). I feel that the
daughter's non-answers dramatize her need for more distance,
whereas the mother, of course, has the opposite need. An all-too-
common dilemma! I've mined my numerous relatives (mother,
father, grandparents, et al.) in short stories as well as poems, but I
realize I've written primarily about the relationships that are
troublesome. The comparatively easy ones may be balm to my
heart, but don't fuel as much creativity.

Tyler Flynn Dorholt

ON THE PRETENSE FOR ARRIVING

The first time my son noticed snow
this year he said, Dad, it's knowing out,
and when he stopped he said, no, it's not-
knowing out. What are we if not indoors?
In the well-lit lift of Amber ale the red
sails around itself. I am here to notice my
consumptions. The evening eye-patch
dies in lint. The child's alphabet
quivers as certain letters grow untouched.
I believe in an alamo still sentimental
about the start of the skirmish—before
the blood, they say, tinkering well past
heartbeat. Tonight it is still not-knowing
outside. Cold rain slays a fact. Reports
are subjugated and we occupy bleachers
of combat for headlines, pretend to have
called out the innards. Paths between moles.
What's that sound, my son asks. I tell him
it's a helicopter but I don't say why. No, dad,
he says, it's not a helicopter, it's going home.

First my snow
this year outs
when stopped.
We know doors
or amber
I am my
evening eye
dying certain
belief. I
start before
I can heart
the outside
fact we
occupy heads
of pretend
paths of
that sound
I see my son say
why it's not
gonna' home.

ON THE PRETENSE FOR REMOVING

In the middle of a run
two deer gush across
my path and I follow them
to where they stand still.
I lean against one of them,
hoping to shoulder its traverse,
but it has bounded away with its
hide, deeper into the woods
and I am alone in the snow.
What meander isn't bled
to its core by the fixity
of the arranged? The red
hedges are hanging on
by the window because
they think there's something
going on. The wind is inside
them. They watch my son
keep his young hands locked
on blocks as he carries
them over to me at the wood-
stove. Smoke slips out of
the chimney and, as snow-
flakes fall, it fades them
into the wet splash of night.

Of a
rush
in me
to where
I lean
one of
shouldering
it is with
the woods
I am
bled
to core
red hedges.
Windows
think
the wind
is them.
Hands
carry
over
the slip
of them
is fading
cool.

ON THE PRETENSE FOR LEAVING

Since I am no longer   *Since*
ending my nights on   *nights spill*
gin, my spiel on truth   *truth*
has begun to thin out.   *is a dream*
I dream of cubeb   *off cracks.*
floating on cracked cubes   *Color*
and the color of juniper   *growing*
growing back inside   *my body*
my body. I can barely   *barely*
answer an email. My eyes   *eyes what*
die in what my thumbs   *cannot*
cannot green—oh orchid,   *fail.*
oh azalea, why my fail?   *Ask a*
I wake up asking my   *mother*
mother if she knows   *she says*
how I am doing and she   *aren't*
says no, how are you,   *you, didn't*
and I say aren't you   *you*
supposed to know?   *provide?*
Didn't I provide signs   *Myself*
of myself way back   *to tonic*
when? I don't answer   *wants*
to tonic or vermouth.   *ships*
I want ship-straight sips   *of*
of something uncouth.   *shots*
When I can't find   *of*
the shoelace I measure   *to be*
my portions by how   *holding*
long my hand can   *while*
be steady while   *holding*
holding myself   *down*
upside down against   *whole.*
the windows.

ABOUT TYLER FLYNN DORHOLT

Tyler Flynn Dorholt is a writer, visual artist, and educator. His most recent books are *Side Cars & Road Sides* (Greying Ghost) and *American Flowers* (Dock Street Press).
He is currently Visiting Assistant Professor at the College of Environmental Science & Forestry in Syracuse, NY, where he teaches, coordinates the Digital Storytelling Studio, and edits the journal *Unearthed*. He is co-founder and editor of the journal and press, *Tammy*, which is now entering its tenth year of publishing. Photograph by Katie LaClair.

ABOUT THE POEMS

About these poems: the false claim is what made me start writing these pretense poems. I am thinking a lot about that line between questioning and claiming, querying and naming. I've been writing poems that are doubled by what falls out of them; redistributed by conscious thinning. I am interested in that which keeps a quieter dangle than the initial and often bulky impulse of my own prose, that which branches rather than trunks.

Melisa Cahnmann-Taylor

"NOTHING'S MORE UNFAIR THAN TO JUDGE THE MEN OF THE PAST BY THE IDEAS OF THE PRESENT"
—*Denys Arthur Winstanley of The University of Cambridge, 1912*

As if history by being history 's
watertight, bullet-
   proofed, clean-handed, flaw-full
but faultless because history

made great movies,
because history's a bad joke:

   Did you hear the one about Jacque Cousteau
    who, to tally fish, exploded a coral reef?

because history was an explorer,
   because that's *just what people did back then*
to fish, to coral, to other

people who were differently
abled, similarly loved, opulently poor.

No one wants to make anyone feel
bad, because one body's sour lock opened,

slurred on soccer fields,
in bank lobbies, overheard
in check out lines,

   I love him, and he's my friend,
   but I don't know what to do with him. He's
    a freak of nature.
           Her,

she likes to be called "her," referring
            to a small town neighbor whose slip's
                        always showing, who painted a house

"social butterfly" yellow.   The black belt
conveys the contents of our kitchens;
            credit scanners ask us to accept,

tap *yes* with a stylus
            that only looks like a pen.

This is a woman writing about a man
who wanted to become a woman.

This is about a man who looked like a woman.

This is about a man who looked
like a good man. This is a woman

writing like a man who exploded
silence with dynamite and tallied the losses.

            Just how it was,
                        nothing's to be done.

This is about a girl who says

I'm not a girlie-girl or a tom-boy,
            I'm something in between.

This is about a boy who asks

            why in the movies when a girl goes on a date
            with a boy, parents are worried;
            why don't parents ever worry about the boy?

Youngsters shrug, unsure
who's in charge
of small fiefdoms of pain,

who's picked
            to hold the door open, turn out
the lights, lead
pain at the line's front where its quiet
            squeak slips unnoticed
like a hair tie to the floor, not
like a bad joke:

            What do you call a retarded fruit?

Shh. We tell them. If you don't have something nice to say,

say anything,
            anything at all.

PORA'S DROUGHT SONG

"California leftist legislators are passing new water conservation rules that can only be described as Communist."~ Independent Sentinel, June 2018

Daughter, daughter, bought her water,
      put it in a plastic bottle,
            there she kept it very well.

She marched in a parade of showers,
      watered her delirium flowers,
            rinsed the clothes in big machines.

She'd sent her horses all to drink,
      tapped out tunes by kitchen sinks,
            strum and drummed her rights to fill

doggie troughs, a pool, jacuzzi.
      Come hell or rings around the rosy
            she'd pay less in Mississippi.

At the crematory, flushing fluids through the trees,
      blinding mice in threes,
            she made molehills from disease.

"Commies, commies, go away!
      Wash your violation days
            down a thousand dollar drain!"

Her shores filled up with plastic caps.
      On heaps of trash, she took her naps.
            She sang of just another day

when seas would change to sail it smooth,
      have less humpty-dumpty to prove

            as we ashes ashes

                all   fall   down!

WOULD PORA HAVE TOLD?

The boy who stole cookies from the donation bag,
Or sold books from the donut bag,

the one who hid vodka in suit pockets, the one
who's head rocked to music, pock marked

who lifted dirts or shirts and Pora, willingly, wanting
his thick mouth on her neck: said *thick*, said *mouth*

said *lift*, said *neck*, said *no*. But what would she tell?
Blurry with drink, would she have told

of naughty peeking, shrank a 5'8" flank,
say it was flimflam shenanigans, like words

were dotted lines that no one reads.
No trespass signs that no one sees

when they laughed at her expense,
gaffed fat at her defense. Blame nipples

or eye twitch, ripples or cry *why bitch?*
If she told, bold, anyone, many ones:

        what would she say?
        why would she stay?
        who'd take the blame?
        who'd stay the same?

TREATMENT

I have known the dizzying rush of deep tissue
manipulations on my table; lean, muscular torsos,
young hips and barely breasts exposed, breathing
complaints of pain down sinewy calves through tiny
feet I lifted, like a god, to puckered cabin ceilings, teasing
ungloved fingers at ball and socket joints, measuring
downy beginnings with classic "thrust" techniques
to diagnose, reduce inflamation, prepare for the win.
And I've worn jackets in the team's white satin, cock-
tails with coaches, university presidents, eager-to-please
parents begging for my time to poke and prod,
fill medal and trophy cases with gymnasts,
dancers, rowers, runners, swimmers, figure skaters.

ABOUT MELISSA CAHNMANN-TAYLOR

Melisa Cahnmann-Taylor, Professor of Language and Literacy Education is the author of *Imperfect Tense* (poems), and three scholarly books in education. Winner of NEA "Big Read" Grants,  the Beckman award for "Professors Who Inspire," and a Fulbright spent in Oaxaca Mexico, she judges the ethnographic poetry competition for *Anthropology & Humanism*. Her work has appeared in *Georgia Review, American Poetry Review, Women's Quarterly Review, Cream City Review, Barrow Street, and many other literary and scholarly homes.* She posts at her blog http://teachersactup.com.

ABOUT THE POEMS

I intend to be present to poetry as a gift, a salve, a refuge, a lab experiment. I read and hope the contents of others' poems sifts with the contents of my (sub)conscience as I author my own lyric witness to human and non-human beauty and pain. I seek words for what I cannot yet say, for what I don't understand, for what makes me afraid, angry or swoon. I teach poetry classes as often as I can and I commit to giving my students writing invitations that I, myself, would like to receive. I believe in writing alongside poetry instruction because students energize me with authenticity and keep me accountable to clarity and what my own shiftings aesthetics are becoming. I prefer a tribe of those who can access more than one language, race, gender, culture, religion, (dis)ability, or other hue of living that helps expand and question what I think of as normal, appropriate, and possible. I read the news like a poet, trying to understand what makes a person abuse their power or share it. The surprise that awaits in a new poem is, for me, a form of prayer for healing myself and perhaps a small piece of the world.

Poets from the Le Moyne College Creative Writing Program

It was an honor to be asked to judge poetry competition of the Newhouse Awards at Le Moyne College this year, and it was a pleasure to read so many good poems that were submitted by undergraduates in the program.

The Newhouse Writing Awards are presented annually as a way of recognizing the best work of Le Moyne college students in five genres – creative nonfiction, critical essay, poetry, short fiction, and play, film or television script. My part was the poetry, and I thought to share here some of the poems that struck me as particularly interesting.

Here are some brief notes on the poems I chose for this selection:

Meghan Lees' "Venice" was enchanting and unexpected in its use of language as a set of casual, conversational couplets in what amounts to a ballad with a repeat chorus. Her tone is consistent, the melodies clear, the words appropriate, the rhymes unobtrusive. A real success. The second poem is not a rhyme but a hate ballad, "A Love Poem To Someone I Hate." Hate poems are pretty much irresistible when done as well as this one is.

I love the journey in Alyssa Goudy's "I Am: Divulging into Self Wonder, " from "I am chaotically optimistic" to "I am the girl of light." In between those two points we get an abbreviated anatomy of the world: sea-turtles, honeybees, dogs, mountains, flashlights, hurricanes, library, books, flashlight beams… Wonderful! The images are handled nicely in the world of the poem, which is to say, they all fit, they develop organically, while the rhythms of the long lines maintain tension and heft, not an easy thing to do even for poets who have been writing for a long time. Another very good piece of work.

AnnMarie Wood's "Music Box" is tightly designed, its language intricate. The opening line, "Harvest gold winding key" launches the music box with a nice imitation of the slowed and careful act of winding the box. The syllables come slowly to the mouth in this line, as they come more quickly in the line "Rotating pins pluck the notes…" It is a good ear that moves through these changes just so, dancing throughout until it reaches "double-time," then slows to the last two lines with the remembrance of time again (the horologist being both the theorist and the maker of watches).

I like the musing, meandering way Andrew Wrede's "The clock ticks by" forms, combining the urgent and the casually seen in a carefully built edifice as it deals with the aftermath of a love affair. Consider the first stanza: "The clock ticks by glowing white / the hand about to turn 9. / The rain reflects red light off the sidewalks / and the time to call you has passed, / the bridges still singed, rotted and ready to collapse." Clock to sidewalks to a forgone opportunity to do something to connect with the lover, shown in the clever rhyme of "passed" and "collapsed." The ancestor of this construct is Apollinaire's "Zone," where interior and exterior worlds collapse and reflect each other, the thing and the thing seen become one gesture.

The vignettes in Natasha Beauchesne lovely "Geology" and "Snake" attracted me to the poems. The kids seeing the rock in the front yard as an asteroid from Paleolithic times, the speaker and her friend surveying the world from the edge of the earth, until the friend's mom calls them back inside, and the fantasy ends: nice. "Snake" forecasts its story of a love gone wrong in the first lines: "I told him I liked his voice, which was true but / a mistake." The statement rightly colors the rest of the poem, as we move from seductive sibilants to lovemaking's unsafe moment, when the word "sincere" is the one the faux lover chokes on.

Molly Murphy's "I would call you butcher, but that wouldn't be right…" has one of the most inventive and honest titles I've ever seen, because as striking as it is, the poet confesses that she is actually the one at fault, "slaughtering myself, / slicing up my own heart, / wrapping it up in white paper / and passing it to you." This is a confessional poem but also a poem of realization and redemption, fierce and brutally honest, and well done. I admire its honesty and craft, the way it lets loose, opening itself to the unpleasant world of grisly images, and then returning to the weight of bearing her own life and to the promise of hope. At the end she has not got rid of his memory, but is working on it.

Readers will find other virtues in these poems than the ones I mention here, but I wanted to give a sense of what attracted me to them. Unfortunately, not everyone can win the poetry prize this year, but every person who submitted for the contest writes with a sharable and radiant joy. Their poetry is for everyone.

—Bob Herz

Meghan Lees

VENICE

Cobblestone kisses my feet and the sun beats
Down on my wind chilled cheeks
We are drenched in color on sight
Proven completely wrong and yet completely right

And You are a completely different story at night

Bleeding ink through pages of my beating heart
Putting us together as you're torn apart
Clouded conversations streaking down a dark
Alleyway like a stark white light

You are a completely different story at night

We peak and valley
We slowly stall
We whisper to the lights

You are a completely different story at night

A LOVE POEM TO SOMEONE I HATE

Get a flat tire on the way to work and
I'll sing a ballad to the sharp edge of glass
If your printer is jammed I will
embrace the paper lodged inside
When you get called into work I will
kiss the phone as it rings
If your power goes out I'll
buy coffee for the fallen tree branch

and
remember the days
that I cried on the subway
And you flung your arms out and
Offered a rose to my tears and
Wrote a poem for my struggle and
Made love to my insecurities because
all you had to do
was turn the lights off.

Alyssa Goudy

I AM: DIVULGING INTO SELF-WONDER

I am chaotically optimistic
I wonder how baby sea turtles are born with the courage to swim
    from sandy shorelines to the depths of the ocean
I hear the harmonious buzzing of honeybees whizzing in my ribcage
I see forests and mountains and oceans and skylines and castles and
    open fields and lots of dogs
I want to embark on the greatest adventure of my life, but how can
    you leave your roots— the people that grew you with love until
    you could finally bud and bloom
I am the girl in the garden

I pretend I am made of flashlight beams, shining through my
    darkest days
I feel all my windows are half open and I'm still trying to decide if I
    want to lock the door
I touch his hands and understand how hurricanes dissolve into
    drizzles of rain
I cry for the good times, the bad times… and the "every-times"
I am the ethereal shine of twilight

I understand that darkness nefariously weaves and unweaves herself
    into the hearts of others
I say words found from all of the corners of my library hoping my
    metaphors and stories mean something someday
I dream of drowning in the ever pleasant world of books
I try counting my day in dogs to make the time pass a little quicker
I hope to build gardens, and bookcases, and surround myself in the
    gloriously enchanting world of books and bumblebees
I am the girl of light

AnnMarie Wood

MUSIC BOX

Harvest gold winding key
shimmers as it twirls.
Rotating pins pluck the notes
of a monophonic melody.
Ballerina spins in sync
while dancing in double-time.
The closing cadence remembers
the horologist's design.

Andrew Wrede

THE CLOCK TICKS BY

The clock ticks by glowing white
the hand about to turn 9.
The rain reflects red light off the sidewalks
and the time to call you has passed,
the bridges still singed, rotted, and ready to collapse.

I walk out Alexandria's library late at night,
the front wall mostly windows
letting me see the quiet night.
I spent too much time here after
not telling my parents and your transfer out.

In my left boot's a penny and it brings away the grey;
my foot getting blisters but soaking up my depression,
keeping me out of my room and the library.
I walk down the sidewalk and light posts with
banners run all the way to the clock.

I stand on one side of the river valley,
if I go down I can see the river's beach
and catch a glimpse of Champlain sailing by,
before Stuyvesant's handover and when this valley still spoke
     Dutch.

Down at the beach there was no one, and still the slightest tinge of
     red in the sky. Small waves crashed on steel toes and the moon
     reflected over the river leading a path of light to the other
     shore.
The stars were falling leaving trails of light in the sky where they
     seem to form the dense fog on the shore.

I saw an apparition with a generic face forming out of the mist. The
     old wives tale I heard was true about this place.
My Grandpa always told us never to go here past dusk, let alone 10
     at night.

"Don't you recognize me, I always watched you as a infant when
   your mom was at work. You don't remember your Uncle
   what's his face?" said Uncle what's his face. He asked me how
   me and my sister were doing before he started to dissipate.

I walked faster as if the beach were longer until I had to turn back.
The waves from the water treatment plant around the bend crashed
   on the shore faster and faster. The rhythm it made only
   reminded me of you and me. Of your transfer across the river
   to some prestigious school I could make out on the other side
   of the shore now.
Of your love of Gupta and Roman architecture, or the large
   swathes
 of lost generation poets you memorized. Or the way your long
   eyelashes looked illuminated by the parking lot lights when I
   told you it wouldn't work.
The bridge the bright moon had displayed was swallowed by the
   oncoming mist.
I saw our silhouettes intertwining out of the steam the river's
   foundries emitted.

I would've told our friends, I wouldn't have kept it a secret. We
   used to stay up all night talking. You told me about your family
   gasping for air when your McMansion was underwater in '08
   while I told you about my dad's type 2.
Why you ever went for me, someone with so few interests I'll
   wonder till I'm wise.

I got a 3.9 once you left. It's been six months since I've seen you
   and I've never forgot.
I took the penny out my boot and started up the hill. It was dawn
   and I had to be at the checkout counter by 8. It wasn't worth it
   to go to sleep.

The night holds its grip on me till the morning masks it all again.
So I'll continue this fate and bring back all the books perpetually,
and wait to see some face through the bookstacks
that loves paperbacks as much as you.
Maybe then I'll be over you.

Tasha Beauchesne

GEOLOGY

The rock in your front yard was a boulder,
an asteroid,
a remnant from when dinosaurs
(or maybe aliens)
ruled the world.

Our heads bumping the sky,
we would survey the pavement,
swinging our bruised summer-sunned legs,
imagining we sat
at the edge of the earth.

The evening August sun winked behind the mountains,
sparkling off the hood of your dad's parked car,
lighting the scuffed wheels of our Razor scooters
lying haphazardly in the grass.

We waited for the explorers and the scientists,
with flimsy brushes and microscopes,
to show up and declare our rock a wonder.

With the six o'clock news glowing purple in your living room,
your mom called us back inside.

SNAKE

I told him I liked his voice, which was true but
a mistake. I told him it was something about his s's,

the way he spun the sound from his lips and
curled and dropped words like delicate spirals,
each syllable like seashells,
like the silver of the bracelet
slipping down his right wrist.

He whispered "shhh" to me like I was a
spooked horse--nothing but the whites of my eyes,
the flaring of my nostrils.
I became something to tame.

It was those s's that circled goosebumps
on my skin as he slid fingers
up my thigh and pressed my hand
against his pants.

Silently, I listened to those
silken s's which sounded so sweet in his mouth:
smart,
sexy,
special.
He didn't include safe.

The only word he choked on
was the word sincere.

Molly Murphy

I WOULD CALL YOU A BUTCHER, BUT THAT WOULDN'T BE RIGHT

In truth, I was the one slaughtering myself,
slicing up my own heart,
wrapping it up in white paper
and passing it to you.
I ripped open my ribcage,
offered you handfuls of bloody tissue
from the gaping hole,
and called it love.
You were all too grateful to sink your teeth into me,
letting my blood run down your chin,
pool in the hollow of your throat.
When you smiled, it thrilled me to know
that the red on your teeth was mine.
I cannibalized myself to see that smile.
I licked my wounds raw for another taste of you.

I gave you pieces that I will never grow back.

But now time has passed and I am still starving.
I am searching for untainted meat in a world of carnivores.

I live with my nervous system externalized on a wall,
red thread, photographs, my mind
flayed open and on display.

I want to carve you out of my cells,
I want to scrape every trace of you out of my bone marrow.

No matter how many times I wash my knives,
or how much bleach chases you down the drain,
I will never go back to the way I was before.

I want every whisper of you gone.
I want the pieces of me back.

About The Poets

Meghan Lees ("Venice" and "A love poem to someone I hate") is a Junior with a Theatre major and a minor in Creative Writing. She has always had a deep appreciation for poetry and that it allows her to explore language and paint with words. In the future she hopes to continue to use her poetry as a form of expression that can hopefully bring joy and catharsis to others.

Alyssa Goudy ("I Am: Divulging into Self Wonder") is a first-year student studying English and Theatre. She writes poetry and short stories, and was the recipient of her high school (*John C. Birdlebough*) Senior Keys in English and Music. Alyssa thanks Lisa Spereno and Dr. Ann Ryan for their guidance into the literary world. She lives outside Syracuse, NY, with her parents and younger siblings.

AnnMarie Wood ("Music Box") studies English with a concentration in Creative Writing. She is expected to graduate in December of 2020 with a BA. She graduated from Onondaga Community College in the December, 2017, as a Fine Arts major with a concentration in Ceramic Sculpture. Whether it is visual art, poetry, or prose, Wood often reflects on childhood nostalgia and its relation to the human psyche. While going to college full time, Wood also works two part-time jobs, is the president of the feminist "Making Herstory" club at Le Moyne College, and is heavily involved in volunteering in her hometown: Syracuse, NY. Wood will continue her graduate education in TESOL to help refugees and immigrants coming to America become literate in listening, speaking, reading and writing English

 Andrew Wrede ("The clock ticks by") is a senior and will graduate in May (hopefully).He grew up in Delmar south of Albany, NY, and majors in History. While a voracious reader, he did not write until his sophomore year of college. Other works include publication of the poem "Mississippi Rising" in the 2017 issue of the Le Moyne *Salamander*. Other interests include music, reading, and politics.

 Tasha Beauchesne("Geology" and "Snake") is from Dalton, MA. A junior, she is studying English with a concentration in creative writing and a minor in psychology. She is an editor for Le Moyne's creative writing magazine, *The Salamander*, and is the president of English Club. Currently, she is working on her Integral Honors thesis, focusing on the relationship between literature and eating disorders.

 Molly Murphy ("I would call you a butcher but that wouldn't be right") is a student in the class of 2020 pursuing an English and Communications dual major with a concentration in Creative Writing and minors in Advanced Writing and Arts Administration. She has been writing poetry since high school and hopes to one day work in the publishing industry. She enjoys exploring themes of power, violation, and monstrosity through her writing and is beginning an undergraduate Honors thesis examining those tropes in Medusa and contemporary horror film. She is the Editor in Chief of *The Salamander*, Le Moyne College's student literary journal, and News and Features Editor of *The Dolphin*, the student newspaper.

Congratulations to Le Moyne College
Newhouse Award winners:

Newhouse Writing Award in Poetry:
Meghan Lees for "Venice"

Newhouse Writing Award in Any Genre:
Alyssa Goudy for "I Am: Divulging into Self Wonder"

Review: *Collected Poems* by Robert Bly

Collected Poems, Robert Bly (W. W. Norton & Company; 2018)

By Steve Kuusisto

1.

I first met Robert Bly in 1977 when I was twenty two years old. I was half blind, neurotic, and only a few years out of the hospital after a suicide attempt. In those days I had coke bottle glasses and weighed 115 pounds. I could see a pine cone or a Chinese fan when I raised them to my nose but I walked fast since movement hid my shame. Now there was Bly towering over me in the Syracuse airport, the man whose poems I'd read in the psychiatric ward—whose work hadn't exactly saved me but had certainly tripped some switches.

I'm now a 63 year old poet, essayist and teacher whose interest in poetry occurred overnight in a story familiar to thousands of writers and book lovers: hospitalized, deeply depressed, a local writer named Jim Crenner handed me a book by Robert Bly, *Silence in the Snowy Fields.* No one can say where the secret road connecting soul and human reason will take us but young people who are "in extremis" need someone to tell them the road exists. My teacher Jim gave me Robert Bly and in turn I stumbled upon this poem:

Poem In Three Parts

I
Oh, on an early morning I think I shall live forever!
I am wrapped in my joyful flesh,
As the grass is wrapped in its clouds of green.

II
Rising from a bed, where I dreamt
Of long rides past castles, and hot coals,
The sun lies happily on my knees;
I have suffered and survived the night
Bathed in dark water, like any blade of grass.

III
The strong leaves of the box elder tree,
Plunging in the wind, call us to disappear
Into the wilds of the universe,
Where we shall sit at the foot of a plant,
And live forever, like the dust.

As Auden would say, "if I could tell you I would let you know"—since it defies emotional candor to share what these lines meant to me. By the time I was 17 I was so thoroughly ashamed of my disability and so mindful of my losses where the adolescent world was concerned that I decided quite literally to starve myself. Boys of course can be anorexic as we now know, but back then hardly anyone understood this. I found I could take control of disappearing. Soon I weighed 96 pounds, all hip bones and ribs and sunken eyes.

There was the poem: the exact opposite of blunt edged instruments. I didn't know phenomenology. I'd no familiarity with objective correlatives or the deep image. That there should be joyful flesh was news. Only later would I encounter Williams' lines from Asphodel: "It is difficult/to get the news from poems/yet men die miserably every day/for lack/of what is found there." No I didn't know these things. What I found straight away however was the intoxication of possibilities: my inner life was not so barren or lonesome as I'd supposed.

After greeting Jim Crenner in the terminal Bly looked at me and said: "I think you've come from a great distance to be here." Then he added: "You've come down a long road."

2.
Only poetry can show us the soul's propriety. Only poems can tell us solitude and sweetclover and the victory swallows are equally parts of the soul. The soul has its own road and if you're lucky someone gives you a collection of poems that puts you back in touch with your proper wonder though it's likely a lonesome affair. Reading Robert Bly's *Collected Poems* I see again how much he's a poet of loneliness. Sartre said: "If you're lonely when you're alone,

you're in bad company." Bly is never in bad company. Again from
Silence in the Snowy Fields:

Hunting Pheasants in a Cornfield

I
What is so strange about a tree alone in an open field?
It is a willow tree. I walk around and around it.
The body is strangely torn, and cannot leave it.
At last I sit down beneath it.

II
It is a willow tree alone in acres of dry corn.
Its leaves are scattered around its trunk, and around me,
Brown now, and speckled with delicate black,
Only the cornstalks now can make a noise.

III
The sun is cold, burning through the frosty distances of space.
The weeds are frozen to death long ago.
Why then do I love to watch
The sun moving on the chill skin of the branches?

IV
The mind has shed leaves alone for years.
It stands apart with small creatures near its roots.
I am happy in this ancient place,
A spot easily caught sight of above the corn,
If I were a young animal ready to turn home at dusk.

The signature of Bly's midwestern Romanticism is not so much
the alchemy of Jung or the mysticism of Kabir as the simple matter
of walking alone. His lake district is Minnesota. In Bly's poems
walking in solitude tends toward creation. There's always a
reminder of Keats: "If poetry comes not as naturally as the leaves
to a tree it had better not come at all." Though it's not always the

case, in many of his poems Bly refuses company—the better to be
attentive to the things around him:

The dusk has come, a glow in the west, as if seen through the
isinglass on old coal stoves, and the cows stand around the barn
door; now the farmer looks up at the paling sky reminding him
of death, and in the fields the bones of the corn rustle faintly in
the last wind, and the half-moon stands in the south.

Now the lights from barn windows can be seen through bare
trees.

(from "Sunset at A Lake")

3.

I must describe the 17 year old reader who found these lines—
who read them with one functioning eye aided by a magnifying
glass, read them alone in a ward. The boy was experiencing his own
ars moriendi but he knew how to concentrate. Everything was clear
to him. Outside his window Boy Scouts raised and lowered the flag
mornings and evenings and he thought of how clean and noble they
were and he thought of ghost-patients hovering in shadows and the
bright cruelty of springtime roses. He thought of the hospital as a
palace of sorts with its high court and ceremonies. He was
improbably alive in blue April.

Bly is not an adolescent poet. He's more like his friend James
Wright who aimed to write the poetry of a grown man. Yet he is a
poet of uncommon clarity. It's the clarity of Wordsworth and
Shelley:

Love Poem

When we are in love, we love the grass,
And the barns, and the lightpoles,
And the small mainstreets abandoned all night.

Here is Shelley:

The fitful alternations of the rain,
When the chill wind, languid as with pain
Of its own heavy moisture, here and there
Drives through the gray and beamless atmosphere.

Here is Bly:

A Late Spring Day in My Life

A silence hovers over the earth:
The grass lifts lightly in the heat
Like the ancient wing of a bird.
A horse gazes steadily at me.

Or:

Watering the Horse

How strange to think of giving up all ambition!
Suddenly I see with such clear eyes
The white flake of snow
That has just fallen in the horse's mane!

With the publication of Robert Bly's *Collected Poems* I see again
what I first loved and honor the blind young man who ached to
know the astonishments of the local and the affirmations of
mindfulness.

4.

I said I would carry Bly's suitcase to the car. Jim Crenner
walked ahead talking of Lorca and I, all one hundred something
pounds of me, dragged a World War II vintage leather strapped bag
loaded with books. I was shocked by the weight of the thing and
ashamed I couldn't lift it. The men in front of me never noticed.
When at last we got to the car I was bathed in sweat. As we drove
he spoke of Neruda, Yeats, Akhmatova, Whitman, Rumi, and

spoke of them with an intimacy that was remarkable. For Robert Bly poets were secret friends. In the Collected one sees this tenderness brought forward in remarkable ways.

Wallace Stevens and Florence

"Oh Wallace Stevens, dear friend,
You are such a pest. You are so sure.
You think everyone is in your family.

It is you and your father and Mozart—
And ladies tasting cold rain in Florence,
Puzzling out inscriptions, studying the gold flake.

As if life were a visit to Florence,
A place where there are no maggots in the flesh,
No one screaming, no one afraid.

"Your job, your joy, your morning walk,
As if you walked on the wire of the mind,
High above the elephants; you cry out a little but never fall.

As if we could walk always high above the world,
No bears, no witches, no Macbeth,
No one screaming, no one in pain, no one afraid.

Rereading Bly I see a discursive affection in many poems. Here he is, describing the late poet William Stafford:

With small steps he climbed very high mountains
And offered distinctions to persuasive storms,
Delicacies at the edge of something larger,
A comfort in walking on ground close to water.

Something large, but it wasn't an animal snorting
In a cave, more like the rustling of a thousand
Small-winged birds, all together, comfortable,
In a field, feeding. One felt at home nearby.

There are many possible ways to see the world
(To whom we should be fair). When someone
Spoke, his face thought, and his eyebrow
Said it. The words weren't always comforting,

But calculated to nudge us along to that place
—Just over there—where we would be safe for the night.

Like many readers of American poetry I thought I knew this
poet but the *Collected* offers a hundred reasons why I did not.
Robert Bly's voice is more cagey than I'd come to think it. The later
poems have nuance and scruple about too many things to name but
here are a few carefully chosen examples.

My Doubts on Going to Visit a New Friend

"I'm glad that a white horse grazes in that meadow
Outside your kitchen window; even when it rains
There's still someone there. And it rains often
In the mountains.

I have to ask myself what kind of friend I can be.
You'll want to know whether I do dishes,
Or know my share of stories, or any Wallace
Stevens poems by heart.

I know that I won't talk all the time, or steal
Money, or complain about my room,
Or undermine you, or speak disparagingly
Of your family.

I am afraid there'll be a moment when
I fail you, friend; I will turn slightly
Away, our eyes will not meet, and out in the field
There will be no one.

—*For John*

One might call this intimate, proleptic honesty. We are never what we seem and no honest person can blink this away. It's a misreading to see Robert Bly as a poet of innocence. Often he is at his best when addressing himself:

Paying Attention to the Melody

All right. I know that each of us will die alone.
It doesn't matter how loud or soft the sitar plays.
Sooner or later the melody will say it all.

The prologue is so long! At last the theme comes.
It says the soul will rise above all these notes.
It says the dust will be swept up from the floor.

It doesn't matter if we say our prayers or not.
We know the canoe is heading straight for the falls,
And no one will pick us up from the water this time.

One day the mice will carry our ragged impulses
All the way to Egypt, and at home the cows
Will graze on a thousand acres of thought.

Everyone goes on hoping for a good death.
The old rope hangs down from the hangman's nail.
The forty-nine robbers are climbing into their boots.

Robert, don't expect too much. You've put yourself
Ahead of others for years, a hundred years.
It will take a long time for you to hear the melody.

5.

I'm amused by Bly. Amused by his generosity. Who knew that munificence would vanish from poetry during these past forty years? If I could ask that twenty two year old struggling with a suitcase if he thought this would happen—that our poetry would become tacitly disinterested in the unconscious, ironic and often ungenerous, he wouldn't have known what I'm talking about. He'd have chattered happily about poetry as animation, dreams as liberty. He loved the early Bly. I wish I could tell him of the pleasures as Robert Bly matured. He becomes a contrarian about the assured self, something Americans often can't seem to do. I'll close by quoting "Longing for the Acrobat":

> There is so much sweetness in children's voices,
> And so much discontent at the end of day,
> And so much satisfaction when a train goes by.
>
> I don't know why the rooster keeps on crying,
> Nor why the elephant lifts his knobby trunk,
> Nor why Hawthorne kept hearing trains at night.
>
> A handsome child is a gift from God,
> And a friend is a vein in the back of the hand,
> And a wound is an inheritance from the wind.
>
> Some say we are living at the end of time,
> But I believe a thousand pagan ministers
> Will arrive tomorrow to baptize the wind.
>
> There's nothing we need to do about Saint John.
> Whenever he laid his hands on earth
> The well water was sweet for a hundred miles.
>
> Everywhere people are longing for a deeper life.
> Let's hope some acrobat will come by
> And give us a hint how to get into heaven.

**The new book by Nine Mile editor
Stephen Kuusisto.**

"That Stephen Kuusisto enables us to see the world through his blind eyes as well as through the 'seeing eyes' of his dog is this book's amazing, paradoxical achievement."
—BILLY COLLINS

HAVE DOG,
WILL TRAVEL

A Poet's Journey

STEPHEN KUUSISTO

Praise for Have Dog Will Travel:

"Never before has the subtle relationship of a blind person to a guide dog been clarified in such an entertaining way. That Stephen Kuusisto enables us to see the world through his blind eyes as well as through the "seeing eyes" of his dog is this book's amazing, paradoxical achievement."
---Billy Collins

"A perceptive and beautifully crafted memoir of personal growth, and a fascinating example of what can happen when a person and a dog learn to partner with one another."
---Temple Grandin

It wasn't until the age of 38 that Stephen Kuusisto got his first guide-dog, Corky, and they embarked upon a heart-stopping and wondrous adventure. Kuusisto's lyrical prose gives his story a vivid quality, placing us directly into his shoes as his relationship with Corky changes him and his way of being in the world. Profound and deeply moving, this is the story of a spiritual journey: discovering that life with a guide dog is both a method and a state of mind.

Stephen Kuusisto is the author of the memoirs *Planet of the Blind* and *Eavesdropping: A Memoir of Blindness and Listening* and of the poetry collections *Only Bread, Only Light* and *Letters to Borges*. His website is www.stephenkuusisto.com.

The Golem Verses

poems by **Diane R. Wiener**

Available at the Nine Mile website,
ninemile.org, or at Amazon

Praise for The Golem Verses, by Diane R. Wiener:

Poet Diane Wiener unlocks the door to a room of confidences, secrets, passions, and fears. These poems present an interior dialogue in which the Golem is more than symbol or legend but trusted companion and guiding, grounding force. This room is furnished with intellect, wonder, inquiry, discovery, revelation, and release. Curl up in a comfy chair and bear witness to this lyric journey.
—Georgia A. Popoff, author of *Psalter: The Agnostic's Book of Common Curiosities.*

In Diane Wiener's original and fearless debut collection, we enter a dreamscape where Jewish mysticism, childhood games, pop culture and poetry's canon are blended together and all fair game. At its heart is Golem—part advisor, part imaginary playmate, possible lover—a mythical figure who "believe[s] she can be anything" and is playful, wise, and always kind. Wiener welcomes us into a magical, mystifying world that is somehow also intimate and familiar. "Tie the bows," she generously tells us, "hem your brushed brown trousers. Lean in, I'm here."
—Ona Gritz, author of the poetry collection, *Geode* and the memoir, *On the Whole: A Story of Mothering and Disability.*

I never knew a Golem until Diane introduced me. Diane's courage in embracing and welcoming the Golem allows us all to travel with them from "believing I was gone, remembering my own life" to "hindsight is rhubarb, associations strawberry preserved stick." What a glorious, wild, courageous adventure and a pleasure to read.
—Jackie Warren-Moore, poet, playwright, theatrical director, freelance writer. Her work has been published nationally and internationally.

Diane R. Wiener is an educator, social worker, advocate, singer, bassist, and artist. She has published widely on issues related to social justice, pedagogy, and empowerment. Diane is the full-time Director of the Syracuse University Disability Cultural Center, and she teaches part-time for the university's Renée Crown University Honors Program. *The Golem Verses* is her first full-length poetry collection.

A Little Gut Magic
poems by **Matthew Lippman**

Available at the Nine Mile website,
ninemile.org, or at Amazon

Praise for the new Nine Mile Book, A Little Gut Magic, by Matthew Lippman:

I love this book. These are the most natural poems I've ever read. How they flow. How they touch the heads of thoughts so lightly and lovingly and move on. I say this is as someone who runs from even the rumor of a party: If these poems were people I would so crash their jamboree. "A Little Gut Magic" invents a genre: imaginative decency. Is that a genre or a style? Is this a book or an embrace? In these spikey days of distance and exclusion, Matthew Lippman is trying hard to find room for everyone, and almost succeeds. —Bob Hicok, author of most recently, *Hold*.

The world needs a poetry as loving and lyric, as engaged and ardent, as Matthew Lippman's is right now. Epitomized by deep connected-ness and humanity, each poem reaches out to name our *happiness pain*, to comfort and stir us up, all at once. Generous and available, Lippman's poems establish an intimacy that feels easy, but is born of a hard-won wisdom, fueled by willful optimism. *A Little Gut Magic* is the real thing. Feel it. Trust it. It's a tome for our times. —Tina Cane, author of *Once More With Feeling*

Reading Matthew Lippman's poems feels like having a conversation with a hilarious, brutally honest, and brilliant friend." —Jessica Bacal, *Mistakes I Made at Work: 25 Influential Women Reflect on What They Got Out of Getting It Wrong.*

Matthew Lippman is the author of four poetry collections— *The New Year of Yellow* (winner of the Kathryn A. Morton Prize, Sarabande Books), *Monkey Bars, Salami Jew,* and *American Chew* (winner of the Burnside Review of Books Poetry Prize).

Perfect Crime by David Weiss from Nine Mile Books.

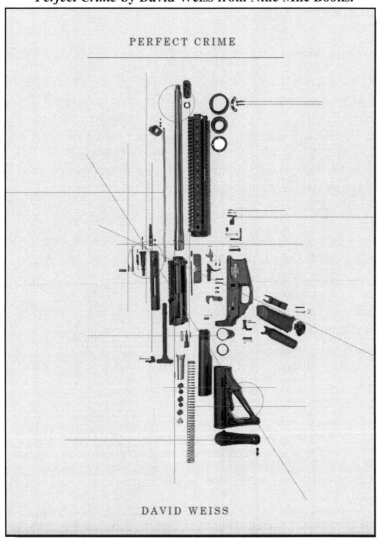

Available at the Nine Mile website,
ninemile.org, or at Amazon

Readers write about *Perfect crime*:

Perfect Crime is a haunted book. In it one feels a pas de deux of despair and obliquity, of image and abstraction. A wry, humorous darkness broods over the pages. Greek myths that thread through the book--Demeter, Andromache, Chronos, Kore, Echo, Hermes and the gang-- imply a larger pattern of doom for humans--humans who have "expiration dates" and are usually crushed in their passionate contacts with gods. In the face of such doom, the human exercise of consciousness, through language, is a brave defiance, that these poems act out in page after page. Perfect Crime feels like one long poem, a "highway / with no exit ramps" and "no exits," coherent in tone and method. — Rosanna Warren

Perfect Crime is brilliant! — Jody Stewart

It seems a perfect example of a poet and poems that make the ordinary extraordinary. And, of course, vice versa. And he does it all with evocative and shifting shades of loss. Also with humor. I was dipping into it and reading various poems, but now I like reading it straight through. I'm the lucky recipient of a very fine collection of poems. — Diana Pinckney

It's an indelible volume. I'm enjoying it greatly. — Diane Weiner